Mystery Tracks in the Snow
A Guide to Animal Tracks

Mystery Tracks
In The Snow

A Guide to Animal Tracks

by Hap Gilliland

Naturegraph Publishers, Inc.

Library of Congress Cataloging-in-Publication Data
Gilliland, Hap
    Mystery tracks in the snow: a guide to animal tracks / by
Hap Gilliland.

    1. Animal tracks—Identification. 2. Tracking and trailing.
I. Title.
QL768.G55   1990
599'.049--dc20   90-5816
                                                           CIP
ISBN 0-87961-198-7: $14.95
ISBN 0-87961-199-5: $ 7.95 (pbk.)

Books for a better world

Naturegraph Publishers, Inc.
3543 Indian Creek Road
Happy Camp, California 96039
U.S.A.

To my mother, Esther Gilliland, who has always understood my love of nature, encouraged my learning about it, and never objected to having a dozen kinds of animals around the house as I grew up.

And to Erma, my loving wife, in appreciation for her patience, understanding, encouragement, and assistance, that make it possible for me to take the trail of adventure, whether I am headed for the frozen tundra, the steaming jungles, or just to a secluded spot where I can write.

Coyote.

Contents

INTRODUCTION

This book is a "fifty year" project. When I was thirteen years old I saw a need for a usable guide to animal tracking, and began writing it. The coyote tracks and pictures of the coyote, wolf, and several other pictures, including the one above, were drawn at that time. Last year, while drawing pictures of wolf tracks in western Alaska, I decided it was time to get all my drawings together and complete this book.

I have generally kept the discussion to descriptions of animals, their tracks, and other visable signs that help with identification. A few stories and experiences are added for interest, and to provide a better picture of what tracking is all about. The book contains the basic information on tracks and tracking needed by a child or adult who has never done any tracking, however, its accuracy makes it a valuable guide for the naturalist as well.

Good luck with your tracking!

Animal Identification

This book is about tracking for fun, but for the student, I have added the scientific name, along with other common names by which the animal is known. I have not tried to list all of the subspecies; only the best known.

The information on the location, or range, of each animal will help in identification of tracks which are very similar.

I have also included the names of some of the animals in the languages of Indian tribes that live in the areas where the animal is common. Most are from tribes in which many of the older people still use the Indian name. In most cases the names are spelled phonetically, using the following pronounciations of the "changeable" letters:

a = ah as in father

e = as in pet

' = glottal (sudden) stop as in oh'oh!

7 = unvoiced L; combined sound of l, t, and th

x or q = a throaty K sound as in German words such as achtung

I had to have the Navajo words written for me. Navajo words have many sounds not found in the English language. Most of us cannot pronounce them.

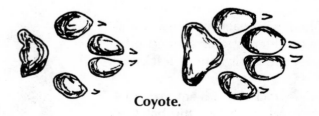

Coyote.

1.

MYSTERY STORIES IN THE SNOW

There are many exciting stories told in the tracks outside your door, but not everyone can read them. Like books, tracks tell their stories only to those who learn how to read them.

I was following the trail of a rabbit when suddenly it ended. The rabbit had vanished as if into thin air. Where could it have gone? Jim fed his cows plenty of corn yet they seemed to be starving. Why? The deer Bill shot was stolen. To get it back, he had to describe the men who stole it and the car they drove. How could he do this when he had seen only their tracks? These are some of the mysteries you will solve as you read this book.

Along with each of these stories, tracks of different animals and other clues for identifying those tracks will be given.

Some tracks tell adventure stories. Others teach us about the habits of the animals that live near us. If people or animals come to visit our homes or camps when we are gone, their tracks may tell us who the visitors were, and even why they came.

Sometimes knowing about tracks can solve a crime or save a life.

To the Indian of the past, learning to track was a necessity. It was his "reading" and if he didn't learn his lessons well he could go hungry because he relied upon his tracking ability to meet his daily needs for food and clothing. But reading tracks was not as simple as reading a book. In a book, each word is printed clearly, and a particular word always looks the same. Tracks are not usually clear and distinct, and there are seldom two tracks that look alike. Parts of tracks may not show, or the tracks may be faint, or changed by wind and sun. Yet the Indian boy had to learn to follow them quickly and without mistake.

Most of us will never develop the skills of our ancestors, who depended on their understanding of nature for their existence, but there are many interesting things we can learn from tracks. Much of what a good woodsman or naturalist knows about the wildlife around him is learned, not from watching the animals themselves, but from following their tracks and observing the evidence that they have left.

Tracking can be useful, but most of all it is fun. It is not just for those who can spend time in the woods. There are many more wild animals around any location than anyone but an expert would realize. Inside any city there are at least a dozen different kinds of wild animals. These may include raccoons, rabbits, squirrels, chipmunks, rats, mice, skunks, weasels, and many others. There are also tracks of dogs, cats, people, and cars, all of which can tell us interesting stories.

There are many opportunities for studying tracks any time of year, but if you really want to have fun learning to track, the best time is in the winter, on a calm day, right after a light snowfall. If the snow is deep, the tracks are hard to identify because they are just deep holes and all look pretty much alike. In summer you can find tracks to study, but you usually cannot follow them far. When there is fresh snow, one to three inches deep, the tracks will be clear, and you may be able to follow an animal several miles and know everything that it did.

But what if you live where it doesn't snow, or if your only chance to go into the woods is in the summer? Don't be discouraged. There are tracks in the mud banks along the streams, in dust, or in sand. Right after a rain, you may be able to track for quite a distance.

Tracking is not just looking at tracks. It is also looking for all the other marks that an animal makes—droppings, gnawings, scratchings, rubbings, diggings, rocks that have been moved, dams, nests, burrows. Often it is impossible to identify an animal from the tracks alone. All these other observations are necessary to give you the clues you need. As you follow the trail, notice the changes in speed and try to determine the reasons for them. Notice what the animal was eating. Learn its life style.

The important thing is to learn to observe, to see everything, and to be aware of what you see, to know its meaning.

You can not learn to track by reading about it, any more than you can learn to play tennis by reading about it. But you can gain information that may be helpful. In the last chapter of this book, you will find some suggestions on drawing, measuring, and making plaster casts, if you are ready to study tracks seriously. For now, read about some mystery stories in tracks and how they are solved.

Look through this book. There are tracks of almost every North American animal to help you with identification. Then, at your first opportunity, take this book with you and go out and observe. Learn to see the signs left by people and animals, and to read those signs.

Whether you live in a big city, on a small farm, or in the Alaskan bush, there are mystery stories in the tracks just outside your door. Will you learn to read those tracks and solve the mysteries they tell?

A.

THE CAT FAMILY

A good place to begin learning about animal tracks is by studying the tracks near home. By observing carefully the tracks of cats and dogs you can learn much that is useful in studying their wild relatives, and the tracks of all other animals.

The cat family has one feature that helps distinguish its tracks from those of other animals. Like the house cat, all the wild cats except the oscelot draw in their claws when they are walking or running. The only time they extend them is when they are attacking an animal, or when they are climbing, or to catch themselves to prevent a fall. Therefore, although the tracks of the cat family look much like those of the dog family, they can usually be distinguished by the absence of claw marks. Remember, however, that tracks are seldom complete. The fact that you see no claw marks does not necessarily mean you are looking at the tracks of a cat, especially if there are only one or two distinct tracks.

Look carefully at the shape. The pads of the cat's feet are usually longer, front to back, than those of the dog, and the toes are grouped a little more in front of the pads. This makes the entire track a little more rounded.

One of the most distinguishing features of cat tracks is their inconsistency. A cat seldom travels far without frequent changes in speed, direction and gait. Walking patterns are very unpredictable.

Cats, both wild and domestic, claw trees "to sharpen their claws." Most of them bury or at least partially cover their droppings.

Except for the jaguar, most cats avoid getting in water.

We are all familiar with the variety of sounds made by the housecat, from the mewing and purring of contentment to the loud meow of the Siamese, and the wail of the tomcat when another enters his territory. The wild cats also have a great range in sounds, and since most of them are night hunters, they are more often heard than seen. Most of their sounds can be identified as cat-like. However, the screech of the mountain lion, which sounds like the scream of a woman, can send cold shivers down a person's back, while the growl of the jaguar sounds more like tearing a piece of canvas.

All cat tracks look much alike. Usually you must distinguish them mainly by the size and the location in which you find them. Size is not always a distinguishing feature either. The tracks of a young lynx may look like those of a bobcat, or those of a young bobcat may look like those of a house cat.

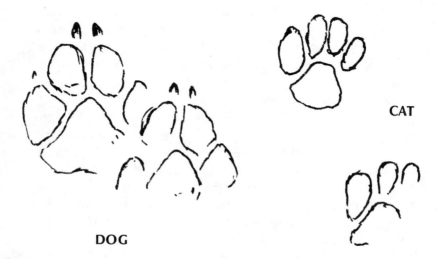

CAT

DOG

Mountain Lion

The range of the mountain lion was once most of North America except the Arctic. They are gone from all but the more remote areas. Tracks are like those of the bobcat but 3 to 4½ inches each way.

MOUNTAIN LION, PANTHER, PUMA, COUGAR: *Felis concolor*
Cheyenne: NaOse'hame (the best of all)
Length: 5 feet plus 3 foot tail
Range: Rockies to the West Coast, and southeast states.

Bobcat

RB

Tracks of the bobcat's hind feet are about 1¾ to 2 inches wide (side to side) and 1¾ to 2½ inches long (front to back). In running, the tracks will usually be in the position illustrated, with hind foot tracks appearing in front of front foot tracks. Walking tracks vary a great deal in pattern, but the most common when walking in a straight line is with the back foot stepping approximately in the track of the front foot as shown.

LB

Bobcats are very important to the balance of nature. As you follow the tracks of the bobcat, you will learn that it can be almost as valuable as the coyote in reducing the number of rabbits and gophers.

Bobcats vary according to locations, from dark to light tan. They have conspicuous small dark spots, and a short tail which is black on top.

RF

BOBCAT, WILDCAT: *Lynx rufus,* and others.
Cheyenne: Mo**hoh**kave (mixed colored)
Navajo: Náá-Isdói
Length: 30 inches, plus 5 inch tail
Range: All of North America except the Arctic.

LF

Tracks shown are from eastern Montana.

Running.

Walking.

House Cat
The tracks of the domestic cat are like those of the bobcat except for their size. The tracks will be 1⅛ to 1½ inches both in width and length.

Lynx
The lynx is an animal of the far north and snowy mountain regions. For walking on snow its feet are larger in comparison to its size, and have more hair than those of other cats. The lynx tracks shown were 3½ to 4 inches each way. Hind feet are somewhat smaller than front feet.

The lynx looks like a very large bobcat except for its tufted ears, black tipped tail, and the fact that it becomes lighter and less spotted in winter.

LYNX, CANADA LYNX: *Lynx canadensis*
Length: 36 inches plus 4 inch tail.
Range: Alaska, Canada, Northern Rockies, Minnesota.

Tracks shown are from Lake Illiamna, Alaska.

back

 front

Lynx

Jaguar

Tracks are like the bobcat's, but sometimes are as wide as 5 inches.

JAGUAR: *Felis onca*
Mexican: El tigre
Yanoamo (South American): Boley
Range: Central and South America, but sometimes gets as far north as Arizona.

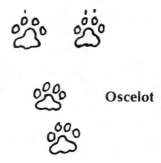

Oscelot

Oscelot

Oscelot tracks are like those of the bobcat but the range is farther south, and unlike all other American cats, the claw marks sometimes show in the tracks. The Yanoamo Indians showed me an oscelot they had just shot with an arrow. The claws were not retracted.

Tracks are about 2½ inches wide.

OSCELOT: *Felis paradalis*
Range: South American rainforest, north into Central America. Tracks drawn in Venezuela.

2.

MYSTERY OF THE RAISED TRACKS

I was crossing a lake on the Alaskan tundra early in the morning on a windy day in March. In the middle of the lake I found the trail of an animal, but it was a strange looking trail. Instead of the tracks being depressions, like other tracks, each track was raised, just as if it had been turned wrong side out. I had once made casts of coyote tracks by filling the tracks with plaster of Paris. When they were turned over, they were raised tracks. That is what these tracks looked like; as if they were casts made of snow and turned upside down. They stood up more than an inch from the smooth ice around them.

I dug into my pack for my paper and pencil and drew the tracks that you see here. I measured one of the tracks. It was almost five inches from front to back!

What kind of wild animal made the tracks? Could it have been a lynx or a mountain lion? An arctic fox?

Why did the tracks stand up above the surface of the ice?

I studied the raised snow tracks. They were obviously shaped like dog or cat tracks. The marks of the claws eliminated any members of the cat family. But the only dogs in the area were sled dogs. They were all chained. Anyway, these five inch tracks were larger than the tracks of a husky. They were obviously the tracks of a large wolf. But why did they

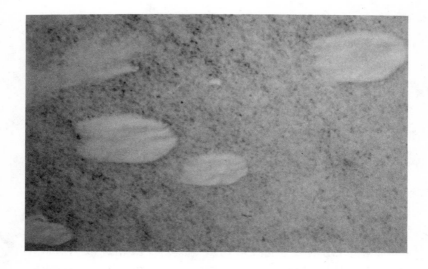

stand up from the snow?

A little study told me the answer. The tracks were made the evening before, when the snow was damp; just right for making snowballs. As the wolf ran across the snow, his weight packed the snow under his feet. When the wind came up in the night, it blew the loose snow off the lake, leaving the packed snow standing up from the ice.

As I followed the trail, it faded out. For a while there was nothing but smooth ice, then the trail appeared again. This time the tracks were neither depressed, like tracks usually are, nor raised like the earlier ones. The ice was as smooth as the ice where there were no tracks; yet the tracks showed very white with dark ice around them.

Why was the track white and the ice dark around it? Try to think of the answer before you read on.

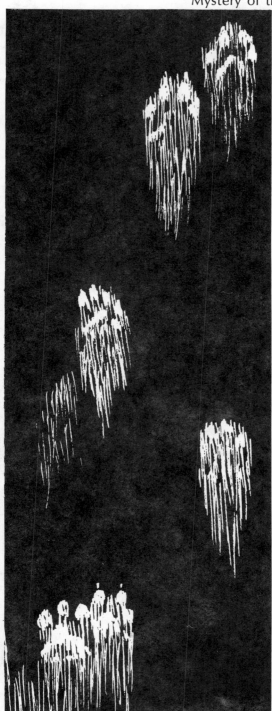

On this part of the lake, the snow and ice had been thawed a little more, leaving the top of the ice a little slushy. As the wolf ran across the slush, the weight of his feet left clear tracks, and compressed the slush around them, making it wetter. As the sun went down, the slush froze into ice, but the wetter part formed darker and harder ice than the rest. Then the wind blew across the lake, filling the tracks with fresh, white snow. The next morning the surface was smooth, but the white tracks were outlined by dark ice.

B.

THE DOG FAMILY

Tracks of all members of the dog family are very similar. The claws usually show, especially if the animal is running. The heel pad usually shows clearly, especially on the front foot. The front track may be wider than the back because the toes tend to spread more, and the pad is somewhat larger.

Since there is such great variety in sizes and types of domestic dogs, it is often hard to tell their tracks from those of their wild relatives.

Track of husky dog. In hard packed sand, only the claws show.

Same husky in loose sand. Life size.

Coyote

Coyote tracks are from 2 to 2¾ inches long and 1½ to 2½ inches wide. The front feet are somewhat larger than the back feet. When running, the coyote's leaps are usually three feet or more—sometimes up to 10 feet.

When tracking the coyote, watch for the leaps it makes when it is hunting mice.

Anyone who has followed the tracks of many coyotes knows how very important the coyote is in keeping the balance of nature. Without it there would be so many gophers and other small rodents in some farming areas that farming would be almost impossible, and jackrabbits would eat up nearly all the grass on many cattle ranches. For this reason, many farmers and ranchers will not allow any coyotes to be killed on their land. However, this is not true in sheep raising country, as the coyote also enjoys a meal of lamb.

COYOTE: *Canis latrans*
Blackfeet: Ah-pi-see
Cheyenne: **O'ko-home**
Cree: Mes-cha-cha-gan-is
Crow: Buate
Oglala Sioux: Mee-yah-**slay**-cha-lah
Length: 3 feet plus 14 inch tail
Range: Originally West Coast to Mississippi River; northern Alberta to southern Mexico. Has moved east and north into more territory as forests were cleared and other predators were killed off.
Tracks shown are from southeastern Colorado.

LB

LF

LF & B

RB

RF & B   COYOTE   RF

trot   lope

front

back

Coyote
1/2 size

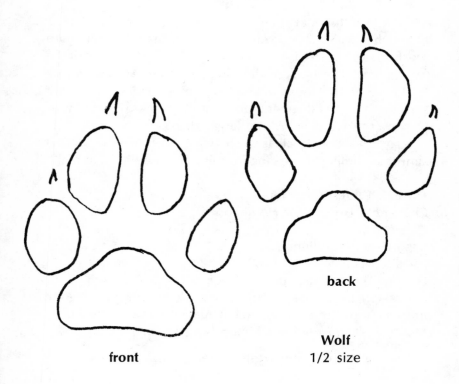

back

front

Wolf
1/2 size

Wolf

Tracks of the Alaskan wolf will be 4 to 5 inches long and 3 to 5 inches wide. This is somewhat larger than the malemute (husky) dog, but size is not a clear distinction as the size of the two overlap. The track of the hind foot rarely shows the full heel pad. The track of the Montana timber wolf is somewhat smaller, though still larger than most dog tracks. The red wolf of New Mexico is very little larger than the coyote.

To run across a clear fresh trail of the Alaskan wolf is almost as thrilling as hearing his deep throated howl at night.

TIMBER WOLF: *Canis lupus*
Cheyenne: Hónehe or Hóniheóo
Tlingit: Gotc
Yupic Eskimo: Kelluneq
Navajo: Má-ii-có "big coyote"
Length: About 4 feet plus 18 inch tail.
Range: Originally most of North America, but wolves are gone from most of the country except Alaska, Canada, the Rocky Mountains, and northern Minnesota and Michigan.

Tracks shown are from west-central Alaska.

Wolf tracks in snow.

Wolf tracks in mud.

Hap G
Age 15

Red fox.

Fox

The tracks of the fox are somewhat smaller than those of the coyote and tend to be somewhat more in a straight line. The individual footprints of the red and the arctic fox will be 2 to 2½ inches long; those of the grey and kit foxes somewhat smaller. The arctic fox track is more likely to show the fur, which covers all of the foot except the pads, while the track of the red fox often shows the mark of a v-shaped ridge across the pad of the foot.

The arctic fox is brown in summer and white in winter. It is much less wary of humans than other foxes. Having found scraps in your camp, it will quite fearlessly come back for more. However, it is not advisable to leave any scraps around your camp, as where the arctic fox lives, there also lives the grizzly bear!

RED FOX: *Vulpes fulva*
Cheyenne: Ma'-hóohe
Cree: Wah-**kus**
Oglala Sioux: Shung-ka-**ge**-lah
Ojibwa: Wah-**gush**
Yupic Eskimo: Kavviaq
Length: 2 feet plus 15 inch tail
Range: Originally all of U.S. and Canada except the west coast, southeast coast, southern plains, and southwest desert. It has now moved into many of these areas. Tracks shown are from central Montana.

Red Fox

GRAY FOX: *Urocyon cinereoargenteus*
Length: About 26 inches plus 13 inch tail
Range: West Coast, Southwest, and from the Mississippi River east. Also Mexico.

Grey Fox

KIT FOX: *Vulpes macrotis*
Length: 16 inches plus 10 inch tail
Range: Deserts of the Southwest

ARCTIC FOX: *Alopex lagopus*
Cree: Wappeeskeeshew
Eskimo: Ka-tug-u-li-a-guk
Length: 2 feet plus 14 inch tail
Range: Northern and western Alaska, and northern Canada. Tracks shown are from Brooks Range, Alaska.

Arctic Fox

snow

loose sand

hard sand

Red Fox

3.

THE MYSTERY OF THE TRAIL THAT ENDED

A light snow sifted down on my shoulders as I skied through the Pryor Mountains of Montana. The snow ended before noon, leaving about two inches of fresh snow on the ground. It was in the middle of the afternoon that I saw coyote tracks in the snow and began following them. They told the kind of adventure story that excites the imagination and makes a tracker glad to be in the great outdoors.

I drew the tracks just as I saw them. The story is all in the tracks on the next two pages. See if you can read it and tell it as it happened.

There are five characters in the story. Can you tell who they are, and what each one did?

To help you tell the story in the right order, I have put numbers, from one to twelve, beside the tracks. Don't look at the solution that follows the drawings of the tracks until you have decided what happened at each of the numbers!

After you have "read" the tracks and told your own version of the story, follow the numbers on the drawing and compare your answers to mine.

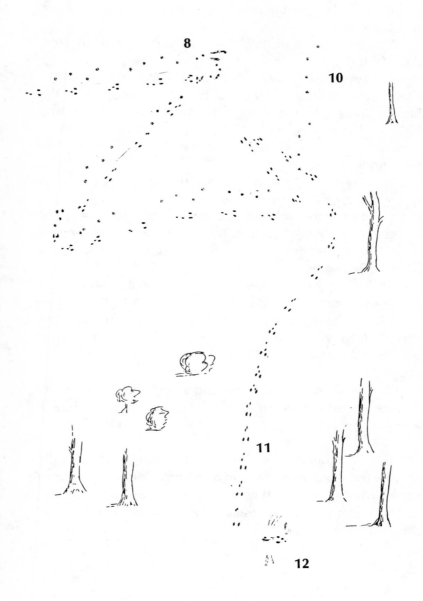

This is how I read the tracks shown on the preceding pages:

1. A small cottontail rabbit was hopping leisurely along.

2. He stopped to look around.

3. A coyote was trotting along when he saw, or smelled, the rabbit.

4. He paused behind some bushes to look.

5. When the rabbit stopped, the coyote leaped over the bushes to catch him, but the rabbit made a big leap forward, digging his toes deep into the snow.

6. A squirrel was digging some hidden pine cones out from under a log.

7. He saw the coyote chasing the rabbit in big leaps across the snow, so he scurried up a tree.

8. The coyote was faster than the rabbit, so the rabbit dodged back, trying to escape. The coyote slid in a wider turn.

9. About that time a cross-country skier appeared on the scene. (That's me.)

10. The coyote saw the skier, so he forgot about the rabbit and made his own escape.

11. The rabbit took off in the opposite direction, but slowed down when he saw the coyote run away. He was so busy watching the coyote he didn't see the danger from above.

12. A hawk swooped down and snatched up the rabbit, leaving no sign but the marks of his wing tips, a spot of blood, and one feather.

Even without the feather for identification, you could assume the rabbit was captured by a hawk, not by an owl or an eagle. Why? (Consider time of day and wing span.)

How can you tell the tracks of the squirrel from those of the rabbit?

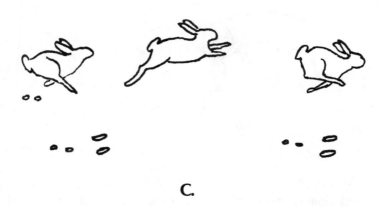

C.

THE RABBIT AND THE SQUIRREL

Rabbits and squirrels are some of our most common animals, and the ones whose tracks you are most likely to see in the woods after a snow.

When rabbits, squirrels, and most other animals run, they run in leaps. As the rabbit comes down, his front feet strike the ground first, but then they leave the ground and the larger back feet pass them, and land in front of the tracks of the front feet, as in the drawings at the top of the page. If you didn't know this, and the tracks were not clear enough to see the toes, you would think the tracks were going in the opposite direction.

Notice that the tracks of the rabbit and squirrel on the following page are going from the bottom to the top of the page. Here, again, the large tracks of the back feet are ahead of the small tracks of the front feet.

Notice also the difference in the position of the front feet of the rabbit and squirrel. Squirrels and most other climbing animals tend to put the two front feet beside each other when they run, while animals that do not climb trees, like the rabbit, usually put one front foot in front of the other. This is often one of your best clues in identifying animal tracks.

When they walk or trot, most animals put the hind foot in, or very near the track of the front foot. The animal picks up the front foot just in time so the back foot comes down in the same track. If the tracks of the back foot are directly on top of the front foot track, they may look as if they were made by a two-legged animal.

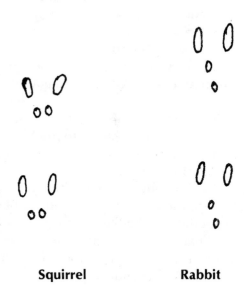

Squirrel   **Rabbit**

Cottontail

Blacktail Jackrabbit

RABBIT

Rabbit tracks are probably the best known and most easily distinguished of all animal tracks. They can usually be distinguished by their position as the rabbit runs, even if any one track isn't clear enough to identify. When the rabbit is speeding, the tracks of the back feet will be farther from the front feet, and each set of tracks will be much farther apart.

If you get a glimpse of the rabbit running away, the tail will help identify which rabbit it is. The cottontail holds its white tail up against its back. The blacktail jackrabbit holds its black tail down. The whitetail jackrabbit holds it straight out or switches it back and forth.

Although rabbit tracks are easy to recognize, determining which kind of rabbit made the tracks is another matter. You may need to use both the tracks and what you know about the different kinds of rabbits and where they live.

Rabbits are born naked, with eyes closed but they grow so fast that the mother can raise more than one litter in a summer. Hares (including the jackrabbits) are born with hair and with their eyes open.

Cottontail

Cottontail rabbits are common throughout the U.S. (at least the "lower 48" states). They are smaller, and have smaller tracks than most other rabbits. A set of cottontail tracks will usually average nine or ten inches from the first to the last track, and unless the cottontail is frightened, the sets of tracks will usually be less than three feet apart.

COTTONTAIL RABBIT: *Lepus sylvaticus*
Cheyenne: Heoue-se'tahe "Yellow feet"
Navajo: Gáh
Length: About 15 inches plus 2 inch tail.
Range: Eastern Cottontail—foothills of the Rockies to the East Coast. Rocky Mountain Cottontail—Sierras to the Rockies. Tracks from southeast Montana.

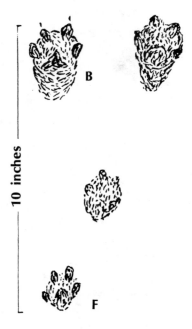

Cottontail Rabbit

Arctic Hare

The arctic hare is similar in size and makes tracks similar to the whitetailed jackrabbit, but its range does not overlap that of the jackrabbit.

It is white in winter except for its black ear tips and yellow eyes. In summer it is grey on the back and white beneath. Along the coast of the Arctic Ocean it stays white all year.

ARCTIC HARE: *Lepus othus*
Chipewyan: Ka-choh
Eskimo: Uka-lik
Dena'ina: Hvaya
Length: About 16 inches
Range: Tundra north of the Arctic tree line or in the alders in such places as the Alaska Peninsula.

Arctic Hare

Blacktail Jackrabbit

Blacktail Jackrabbit

This jackrabbit is leaner, darker, longer legged, and has longer ears than the whitetailed jackrabbit or the snowshoe. It does not turn white in the winter. A set of its tracks will average around 20 inches and the sets will be from one to twelve feet apart.

BLACKTAIL JACKRABBIT: *Lepus californicus*
Cheyenne: Aénoho-vóhkoohe
Navajo: Gáh-có
Length: About 20 inches plus 4 inch tail.
Range: Most of the western plains country from the Sioux country of the Dakotas to the Apache country of the southwest.

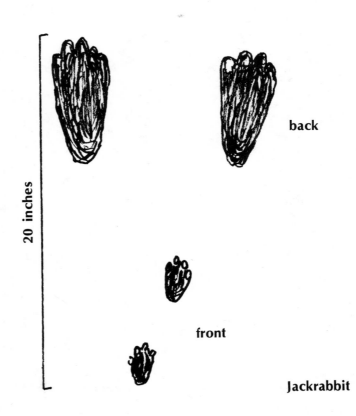

back

20 inches

front

Jackrabbit

Whitetailed Jackrabbit

The tracks of the whitetailed jackrabbit are usually slightly larger than those of the blacktailed jackrabbit. The whitetail is a silvery grey with white tail and underparts. It turns pure white in winter except for some grey on the head and ears. Neither the whitetail nor the blacktail digs a burrow. You will find the spots where they have rested, usually beside a clump of brush.

The whitetail is one of the most solitary of all animals. They are seldom seen together.

WHITETAIL JACKRABBIT, PRAIRIE HARE: *Lepus townsendi*
Blackfeet: Oomk-ah-tsi's-stah
Cheyenne: Vohkoohe (Crooked sitter)
Cree: Mis-tah-boos
Oglala Sioux: Mahs-tin-shkah
Ojibway: Kit-che-wah-boos
Length: About 18 inches plus 4 inch tail
Range: It overlaps that of the blacktail. It may be found anywhere from the Blackfeet and Cheyenne country of the western plains to the high Cascade mountains, and north into Canada.

Snowshoe

The tracks of the snowshoe hare can be distinguished from the jackrabbit's by the very large tracks of the hind feet. In winter thick fur grows between the toes and the toes spread wide when the rabbit runs, making very effective snowshoes. You can identify twigs eaten by the snowshoe in winter by the slanted cut on the ends.

The snowshoe rabbit is also called the varying hare because it turns white in winter except for its black tipped ears. In summer it is reddish brown to dark grey on the back and upper tail, and white underneath.

Snowshoe rabbits multiply very rapidly, and for four or five years there will be more each year, until they are so common that it seems that no matter how many are killed, the number does not decrease. If this continued, the rabbits would eat up all the available food, and they and many other animals would starve. However, during those years, the coyotes and wolves will have larger families and they will live largely on the rabbits. Also, when the rabbits reach a large enough population, an epidemic disease spreads and they nearly all die, leaving only here and there a rabbit or two to start the cycle again.

SNOWSHOE RABBIT, SNOWSHOE HARE, VARYING HARE,
    WABASSO: *Lepus americanus*
Iroquois: Wabasso
Length: About 18 inches plus 2 inch tail
Range: Evergreen forests of Canada, Alaska, and Rocky Mountains as far south as Colorado and as far north as trees grow.

Snowshoe Rabbit
natural size

Squirrel

Squirrels have five equal toes on their back feet, and four fingers and a knob-like thumb (which does not show in the tracks) on the front.

Compare the tracks on the next two pages. It would not be hard to tell the tracks of the squirrel, rabbit, and cat apart if they were as clear as the ones in the drawings, but in the woods they may all just look like holes in the snow. Notice also the difference in the two sets of squirrel tracks shown. Tracks in melting snow may be twice the size of the tracks of the same animal in mud.

When the tracks are not very distinct, identity will have to be based on other clues. The side by side placement of the front feet when running will differentiate the tree squirrel from the rabbit and the ground squirrel, and actions such as going from tree to tree, and stopping to dig up a buried pine cone will certainly separate the squirrel from the cat.

The Red Squirrel and the tuft-eared black squirrel of the Rockies will be found outside any warm winter day, but the grey squirrel hibernates. Its tracks will usually be seen only in an early fall or late spring snow.

RED SQUIRREL, CHICKAREE, PINE SQUIRREL:
   Tamiasciurus hudsonicus
GREY SQUIRREL: *Sciurus carolinensis, Sciurus griseus,* and
   others
Cheyenne: No'kee'e
Choctaw: Fani okchako
Ojibway: Kitchi-adjidamo
Navajo: Lózi-szini (black squirrel), Lozi-Igaii (Grey squirrel)
Length: About 8 inches plus 6 inch tail.
Range: Red Squirrel: forests of most of the United States; likes
open pine forests. Grey Squirrel: eastern edge of great plains
to East Coast. Dense timber areas, hardwoods, near water.
California Grey Squirrel: West Coast. Black Squirrel: Colorado,
New Mexico, Arizona.

Tracks shown are Colorado Black Squirrel.

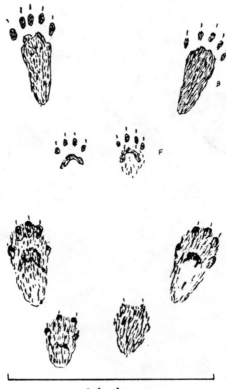

4 inches

Ground Squirrel

There are many kinds of ground squirrels and they vary greatly, from the small, striped, golden mantle ground squirrel of the Rockies to the large grey ground squirrel of the Arctic.

Where both ground squirrels and tree squirrels are present, the ground squirrels are usually somewhat smaller, but the claws are longer and more likely to show in the tracks. The ground squirrels usually put one front foot in front of the other, in the manner of running, rather than the climbing animal.

STRIPED GROUND SQUIRREL: *Citellus tridecemlineatus*
GOLDEN MANTLED GROUND SQUIRREL: *Citellus lateralis*
Blackfeet: Omah-ko-ka-tai-ksi
Dena'ina: Qunsha
Length: 4 to 7 inches plus 2 to 5 inch tail
Range: Different varieties of ground squirrels live in all of the western half of the United States, Canada, and Mexico.

Tracks shown are from Arctic Village, Alaska.

Ground Squirrel

Ground Squirrel

Chipmunk

Chipmunks sleep much of the winter, and also store food in or near their nests, so they are seldom out in the snow. In summer you may find their tracks in mud or dust, or you may see the remains of grass and dandelions or wild oat heads on logs or rocks where a chipmunk has carried them to remove the seeds.

Note that in one of the sets of tracks, the heel of the back foot shows, while in the other it does not. The tracks are about natural size, except that the set of tracks should average eight to ten inches apart.

WESTERN CHIPMUNK, LEAST CHIPMUNK: *Eutamias minimus*
   (one of many varieties)
Blackfeet: See-nah-kah
Cheyenne: Neske'esta (perked ears)
Chipewyan: Thal-coo-zay
Cree: Ches-se-cow-e-pis
Length: About 4 inches plus 4 inch tail.
Range: Rock piles, rocky ridges, stone and rail fences, dry sheltered places. Not deep forest, swamp, or open prairie. Western Chipmunk: Rocky Mountains to West Coast, and Canada. Eastern Chipmunk: Mississippi River to East Coast.

Tracks and photo from Oregon Cascades.

Prairie Dog

It is not likely that you will confuse the tracks of the prairie dog with those of any other rodent. They do not wander far from their homes, and if you are in a "prairie dog town" you cannot miss the mounds of earth that the prairie dogs carefully erect around each of their burrows.

Although other rodents usually avoid the prairie dog town, there will be other tracks. The coyote and the weasel will come to hunt the prairie dogs, and the snake and the owl like to take over abandoned burrows for their homes.

Prairie dogs stay inside on cold stormy winter days, but they often come out and run around in the snow on sunny days in winter.

Prairie dogs were once the most common animals of the plains, but because the land in a prairie dog town could not be farmed, and their holes were a hazard to horses; the prairie dogs were poisoned by the homesteaders in a nearly successful effort to exterminate them. However, there are still a few prairie dogs in each of the states from the Rockies to the Mississippi.

Prairie Dog

PRAIRIE DOG: *Cynomys ludovicianus*
Crow: Tsi'pe
Hopi: Till-keha
Sioux: Ping-sping-sa
Navajo: Łóó
Average length: 12 inches with 3 inch tail
Range: Great Plains: Canada to southern Texas.

The prairie dog.

Gopher

The gopher has short legs and strong front feet with the three middle claws long and well adapted to digging.

The gopher makes a track very much like that of the packrat, but they live in open areas, while the packrat lives in wooded areas.

It is also often confused with the prairie dog, but the gopher is smaller and thinner, and it does not build a protective mound around it's hole.

GOPHER, POCKET GOPHER, PICKET PIN GOPHER:
Geomys bursarius and others.
Cheyenne: Estema'e
Navajo: Naazisi
Length: About 8 inches plus 3 inch tail
Range: Great Plains. Other species throughout the United States.

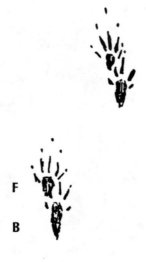

F

B

Cony

The cony is a very interesting, hard working, little animal that looks like a tiny rabbit except that it has small ears and no tail. When you are climbing in rock slides above the timberline you can detect its presence by the grass spread out on the rocks to dry in the sun. In three months of summer, it stores enough of this hay to feed it thorough the nine months of winter. You are not likely to see it unless you hear its squeeking call and look closely at the tips of the rocks, with which it blends perfectly.

Since it lives in the rocks where it does not make tracks, and does not need to come out when there is snow, I have never seen its tracks.

CONY, PIKA, ROCKRABBIT: *Ochotona princeps*
Length: About 6 inches. No tail.
Range: High rock slides in all western mountain ranges that have large areas above timberline.

4.

MYSTERY OF THE TALK IN THE NIGHT

Solving this mystery may save your life if you are lost in the woods!

David and Marie pulled their pickup camper off the road into the forest to camp. It was early spring and there was about three inches of fresh snow on the ground. They crawled into their sleeping bags, and David had just fallen asleep when Marie whispered, "There's someone outside. I hear them talking!"

"There can't be. There's no one within miles." David said. But he cranked the window open and, sure enough, he could hear someone talking not far away. Another voice answered.

"What are they saying?"

"Can't tell. Sounds like someone trying to talk with his mouth shut." David turned his flashlight to shine out into the woods, but he could see no one.

Needless to say, Marie didn't sleep much that night. Twice more, before morning, she heard the voices.

At daylight, David went out exploring the area. The tracks of one rabbit crossed nearby, and the tiny tracks of a shrew wound through some bushes, but David knew those tracks well. He was soon convinced there were no other tracks within several hundred yards of the camper.

David was mystified. He did notice that on top of the snow, around one fir tree there were a lot of green twigs, as if a squirrel had been dropping them. David picked up one of the twigs. It was larger than a squirrel would cut, and there were no cones. A squirrel would cut twigs with cones, then gather the seeds later.

Looking up into the tree, David saw three spots where the bark had been gnawed off the tree, leaving the bare wood of the trunk. Two of these were too high to be the gnawings of an elk or a moose. All were above branches where an animal could sit easily on the limb and gnaw the bark above it, but there were no tracks in the snow around the tree.

Can you solve the mystery? Who was talking in the night? What animal had chewed the bark? How could knowing about it save your life? After you have decided on your solutions, read on.

❀

The voices which Marie heard were porcupines talking to each other! Porcupines have very human sounding voices, and they "talk" in a long series of grunts which raise and lower a great deal in tone and inflection.

Want to know what they sound like? Try keeping your lips tightly closed while you try to say, "Well, well! Look at that strange animal out there!"

A lone porky may talk to himself for a short time in the evening while he eats, but a mother and her young may keep it up most of the night. I have never heard them in the daytime.

A Montana rancher once told me of his trouble with porcupines which were eating the lettuce in his garden, gnawing on his axe handles, and wading through his hay field, tramping it down at night. One of them had seriously injured one of his horses by filling its nose full of quills when the curious horse put it's head down to smell the strange creature.

I took my sleeping bag, flashlight, bow and arrows, and a small rope, and slept in the woods near his garden. About ten o'clock I heard a mother porcupine and two young ones talking to each other. I didn't have to use my arrows as I was able, after much poking them out from under logs, to get all three of them, one at a time, to waddle into the noose of my rope. I dragged them to my car, tossed them—carefully—into the trunk, and hauled them a couple of miles down the road. Then I had to figure out how to get them out of the trunk!

If you find a porcupine, you can easily catch up with it because a porcupine can't run much faster than a man can walk. A snap of a long scarf against its back will give you a good sample of quills to study, but stay far from its tail. The porcupine's tail is lightning quick and well armed. Its quick action is responsible for the false idea that a porcupine can throw its quills.

Porcupine quills contain a poison which causes the wound to remain sore long after the quill is removed.

Slide your fingers along a quill and you will find that it feels very smooth going one way, and rough the other way. This is because of the microscopic barbs all the way along the quill, which make it go in very easily, but make it very hard to pull out. When a quill enters a muscle, every time the muscle moves the quill goes deeper. It can work its way clear through a leg.

Porcupine quills were the main decoration for the clothing of the Indians of the West, until the beads of the white man became available. The Hupa of California wove quills into their baskets, but they got them mostly by trade as porcupines are comparatively rare west of the Cascade Mountains.

Knowing the signs of the porcupine could save your life. In some states there is a law against killing a porcupine except in an emergency for food, because the porcupine is the only animal a person lost in the woods without a weapon can kill with a club.

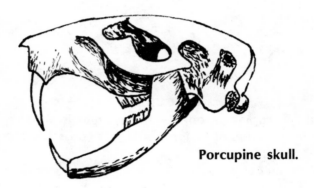

Porcupine skull.

D.

OTHER RODENTS

Rodents form our most common group of wild animals. They are commonly known as gnawing animals because they are easy to identify by the two large front teeth, made for gnawing. These show clearly in this drawing of a porcupine skull, which is similar to the skulls of all the rodents.

Most of the common rodents (but not all) have five toes on the back feet and four on the front. This is one way of distinguishing their tracks from those of the meat eaters. However, except in good snow, it is difficult to know if all of the toes show in the tracks.

Since the rodents put most of their weight on their back feet, and use their front feet to pick things up, their back feet are usually larger and stronger, while the front may be more hand-like. This makes their tracks different from most other animals, because there is no apparent difference in the tracks of the front and back feet of most other animals.

N G
Age 12

Porcupine

The porcupine is one of those animals which leaves plenty of evidence of his presence, but you seldom see his tracks.

In summer you may see a winding trail of bent over grass in a hay meadow, where a porcupine has spent a night wandering around eating weeds. Or you may see him threshing through the brush trying to get away if you walked too close, or you might hear the yelp of your dog if he has not yet learned about porcupines and has gotten his nose full of quills.

In the snow, you may possibly see the trail of a porcupine where he has waded from one tree to another, but you are more likely to see the spots where he has been eating bark.

If the snow is new, and you find a lot of twigs below a tree that have been dropped since the snow, there is probably a porcupine in the tree, but he may be hard to distinguish from a big bunch of limbs and pine needles. If the snow is old, the porcupine may have left, as its trail could have been obliterated by melting. Even so, it is probably in a tree not too far away, but it may take careful observation to find it.

In winter, a porcupine will often spend days in the same tree eating bark as long as there are easily accessible spots where it can perch on a limb and eat. It also likes the tips of the twigs. Usually in summer when the twigs are juicy, but sometimes in winter, the porcupine will cut off large numbers of these twigs and drop them to the ground. It may later climb down and eat these, then sit on the snow and eat bark from the tree trunk. In the spring, the height of the gnawed bark from the ground will tell you how deep the snow was. But life is easy for the porcupine, and it is neither highly intelligent, nor highly motivated. It may never get around to eating the twigs it cut.

If you do find the tracks of a porcupine, you will see that it walks with a waddling gate, with the back feet stepping almost in the tracks of the front feet.

In dust or light snow its swinging tail will make swishing marks between the tracks.

The flat-footed tracks look much like miniature bear tracks. They are about three inches long, and the long claws show plainly. There are five toes on the back feet and four on the front.

With its short legs and heavy body, it plows a deep furrow through soft snow.

PORCUPINE: *Erethizon dorsatum*
Cree: Kahk
Chipewyan: Dthen
Crow: Apári
Oglala Sioux: Sink-pay-lah
Navajo: Dasan
Ojibway: Oga
Length: 18 to 24 inches plus 10 inch tail.
Range: Dakotas to Cascades, New Mexico north; forests of northeastern United States; all of Canada and Alaska except the northern barrens and Canadian plains. They prefer the forests but will also be found on the prairie east of the Rockies, and the tundra of the Alaskan Peninsula.

walking

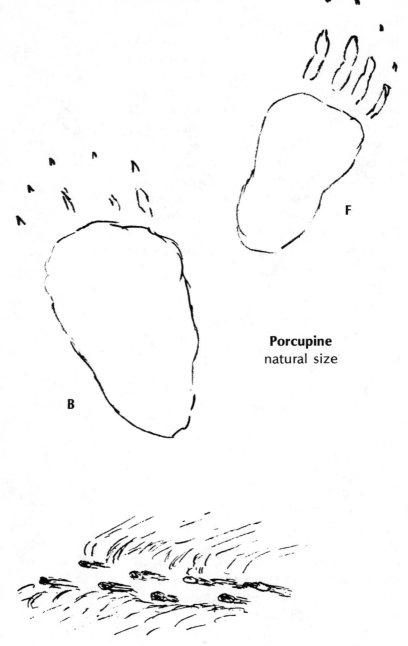

Porcupine
natural size

B

F

Porcupine tracks in deep snow.

Beaver

A beaver trail in deep snow will be a deep groove in the snow like that of a porcupine, and both will have tail marks which partly obscure the footprints. The two may be hard to tell apart until you can find a clear footprint, as the webbed foot of the beaver, although about the same size as the footprint of the porcupine, is easy to distinguish from that of any other animal.

Ordinarily there is no problem identifying the beaver's trail because long before you see the tracks of the beaver you will have already seen the dam, the beaver's house, or stumps such as the ones in this photo.

You will also see cut limbs and drag tracks where the beaver has been cutting aspen, poplar, or birch trees and dragging them to the water.

However, in places like the rivers of the west coast of Oregon and California, where the water is sufficiently deep to make a dam unnecessary, and annual floods would destroy a dam, the beavers do not build dams or beaver houses. Instead they make their home in the river bank by digging a hole with an underwater entrance.

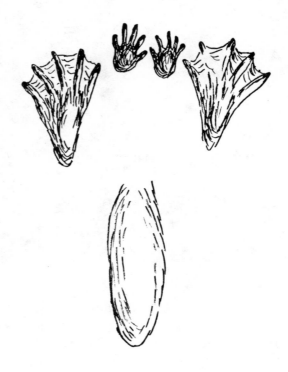

Beaver tracks, sitting.

BEAVER: *Castor canadensis*
Cheyenne: Homa'e
Chipewyan: Tsa
Cree: Ah-misk
Dena'ina: Chu
Oglala Sioux: Chan-pah
Navajo: Caa'
Length: About 3 feet plus 12 inch tail
Range: Originally all of United States and Canada wherever there are suitable trees along streams, except Florida.

Tracks shown are a composite of several partial tracks from the Beartooth Mountains, Montana.

**More of the
beaver's work.**

Packrat.

Packrat

The packrat, or woodrat, is buffy brown on the back, white underneath, and has a bushy tail, which makes it quite different in appearance from other rats.

The packrat, also called the traderat, is named for its habit of "packing" something around with it, in its mouth, which it "trades" for the next thing that strikes its fancy.

Our family once had eight bushels of apples stored in a root cellar. When we went to get some, they were all missing, but each basket was half full of pine cones which the packrats had "traded" for the apples. We found the spot where the packrats had stored the apples, all in perfect condition. How the packrats had managed to carry those apples without breaking the skin on any of them we could never understand.

There is a story of the Colorado prospector who built a cabin in a valley where he had found a few flakes of gold. He shared the cabin with a packrat which often sat watching him from the logs of his wall. Although he searched for a year, he never found much gold and he eventually ran out of food and supplies. One morning he went to get the last of his cartridges from the can where he kept them. Instead of cartridges there were five pebbles. The prospector grabbed the can and threw it at the packrat. As the rocks flew he caught a glint of gold. The packrat had carried five gold nuggets from under the cabin, where the prospector later found his fortune.

The flesh of the packrat is one of the best meats available. Many people have been discouraged from learning of its delicious flavor because of the name "rat" and the musky oder of the live animal, but packrats are considered a special delicacy by the Hopis and the Indians of Northern Mexico.

The packrat likes to build its nest in clumps of cactus, around the base of a tree, in an old cabin, or in a cave in the rocks. The soft nest is protected by a large pile of sticks and cactus, and is decorated with whatever interests the rat, including your silverware if you leave it around camp.

PACKRAT, TRADERAT, BUSHY TAILED RAT, WOODRAT:
Neotoma cinerea
Cheyenne: No'ketse (Stealer)
Hopi: Kee-hua**cahl**-a
Length: About 8 inches plus 7 inch tail
Range: Colorado and New Mexico to the West Coast, and north into Canadian Rockies.

Tracks from southeast Colorado.

walking   **running**

Muskrat

The muskrat's track is like the packrat's, except it is larger and will not be in the same location. Running tracks in snow may look like rabbit tracks except that the tail shows frequently. Unlike the beaver, the muskrat does not have webbed feet.

The muskrat likes marshes and is nearly always near water. He builds his home of reeds or grass on the shore of a stream or lake.

MUSKRAT: *Ondatra zibethicas*
Chipewyan: Dthen
Cree: Was-*usk*
Oglala Sioux: Sink-pay-lah
Ojibway: Wah-**jusk**
Length: About 12 inches plus 10 inch tail.
Range: Wetlands of United States and Canada, except Florida.

Tracks shown are from northern Montana.

Muskrat.

Marmot

Since the marmot or rock chuck hibernates through the winter and lives on the high rocky ridges, you will seldom see its tracks. You will however, know when you enter the marmot's territory by its high shrill whistle with which it warns others of your approach.

YELLOWBELLY MARMOT, ROCK CHUCK, MOUNTAIN WOOD-CHUCK: *Marmota flaviventris*
Cheyenne: Sea-voneske (into-disappearing)
Length: About 18 inches plus 7 inch tail
Range: Rocky places from 2,000 feet to timberline. Rocky Mountains, Sierra Nevada Mountains, Cascade Mountains

Tracks shown are from Berthod Pass area, Colorado.

WOODCHUCK: *Marmota monax*
Range: Canada from Rockies east, and United States from Mississippi River to East Coast.

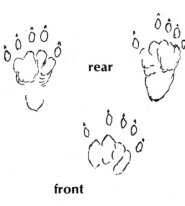

rear

front

Marmot

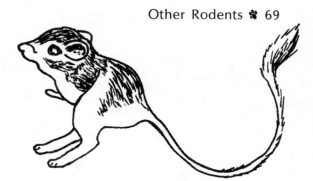

Kangaroo Rat

The kangaroo rat is not a marsupial. It is a rat with well developed jumping legs, which allow it to leap across the ground like a kangaroo. Since it runs with huge leaps, on its hind legs, its tracks are a series of double dents in the sand, with no front feet tracks showing, except where it stops.

Kangaroo Rat

KANGAROO RAT, *Dipodomys ordii*
Length: About 4 inches plus 6 inch tail
Range: Great Plains and deserts of the Southwest.

Tracks shown are from northeast New Mexico.

Field Mouse and Vole

You can seldom tell the tracks of the field mouse or the vole from those of the chipmunk, except by their location, and clues from their actions.

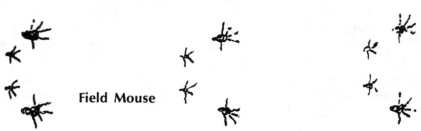

Field Mouse

5.

MYSTERY OF THE MISSING DEER

It was near sunset and Joe's car with the horse trailer was about two miles away. Joe Red Coyote knew he would have to get back to the trailer and head for home, but he hated to make the long drive back to the reservation without the deer meat for the family. He saw a Montana State Patrol car coming, so he stepped off his horse and walked out on the blacktop to flag it down.

"What's the problem?" the patrolman asked as he pulled to a stop.

"Someone just stole the deer I shot this morning," Joe said. "He left about ten minutes ago; headed east. Thought maybe you could stop him. I'm sure he doesn't need the meat as bad as I do."

"It would be pretty hard to catch him," the patrolman said, "unless you know something about him."

"He's a little, short, heavy-set fellow," Joe said. "He's got my deer on top of his car. It's a small foreign car with front wheel drive and new studded tires."

"If the deer's on top of his car he would have to stop at the game check station east of White Sulphur Springs," the patrolman said as he picked up the mike to his radio. When the check station answered, he gave the description, then turned to Joe. "A car like that just pulled into the check station, but there's two men in it, not just one."

"Yeh, I know," Joe said. "The other guy's taller and thinner, but he didn't help steal my deer. He may not even know it's stolen, 'cause he just got to the car in time to help load it on."

As the patrolman relayed the information, he asked, "Know anything else about the driver?"

Joe thought a second. "Well, he's a short pudgy little man, sort of out of condition—never was very athletic. He was carrying a short, light rifle—a 30-30 or something like that—with an open sight. He's wearing knobby soled boots and has mud on the left knee of his jeans. He's limping a little. He was all right when he started out this morning, but he hurt his left foot—or more likely pulled a tendon in the ankle."

The man at the checkstation was back on the air in a minute. "Everything checks out, he said, "but the man insists he shot the deer. The deer tag on it is his. Can you prove it's yours?"

"Ask him when he shot the deer, and if there's anything wrong with it. He'll tell you he shot it this afternoon, but the blood's too dry for that. He won't know the deer has porcupine quills on the inside upper left leg. The leg's all swelled up and festered. He couldn't have missed it if he'd dressed the deer himself. He's carrying a nice sharp knife, but there's no blood on it—or on his hands—and you can tell he didn't wash it off, because his hands aren't as clean as if he had just scrubbed the blood off. They started hunting about seven o'clock this morning, and hunted together all morning, but they split up this afternoon. It was just when they were to meet to go home that the short guy saw my deer and decided to steal it."

A few minutes later the checkstation man was back on the air. "The man admits he found the deer hanging up in a tree, but he can't see how you could have been watching everything he did today without his seeing you."

The patrolman said, "Tie your horse up and hop in. I'll take you down there, and bring your deer back." As Joe got in the car, the patrolman said, "What color did you say that car was?"

"I don't know the color," Joe said, "I didn't see it."

"You didn't see it!?"

"No. Or the men either."

The story of Joe Red Coyote was told to me when I was a small boy, and I never forgot it. I have repeated it here for two reasons. It inspired me to want to learn to be a tracker, and it shows you an example of a good tracker who sees a lot more than tracks.

If you want to figure out how Joe got all that information, you need a few more facts. Although Joe had not seen the men, they had been hunting in the same area all day. There were a few patches of old snow, but it was a pleasant day, until a sprinkle of rain fell about a half hour before Joe stopped the patrolman.

How could Joe have known how many men there were; what time they started hunting; that only one actually took the deer; how long it had been since the deer was stolen; that the man who stole it was short, heavy, not athletic, and had injured his heel; the size of his rifle; that he was wearing jeans with mud on the knee; and all about the car?

Joe could not have gotten all the information after the deer was stolen, but he was observant all day, and he was interested enough to remember what he saw.

As he was hunting that morning, at about eight o'clock he saw the tracks of two hunters crossing a patch of old snow. They were walking quite rapidly up a trail that led from the end of the road, about a half hour away. Although the temperature was only a few degrees below freezing, the snow in the tracks had begun to freeze. Therefore, the tracks had been made about a half hour earlier so the men must have left their car about seven o'clock. The tread on their boots was the same as the men who stole the deer. There might be a question about identifying one pair of boots, but not when the same two were together again.

Although both men wore about the same size boots, and were walking the same speed, one took much shorter steps than the other, and his tracks sank deeper into the mud and

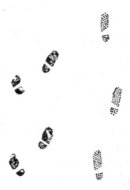

snow. This showed that he was short and heavy. This man walked with his feet somewhat apart, pointed his toes out, and put more weight on the inside of the ball of his foot. He was not an athlete.

In the afternoon, when the weather had warmed up and the mud had thawed, Joe saw the tracks of these men again. They were walking more slowly now, with shorter steps. They had tired quickly so were probably not in good condition. The short man was putting most of his weight on the heel of his left foot and was taking shorter steps with his right. It must hurt when he stepped forward and stretched the Achiles tendon of his left foot—also a common problem with a person who exercises when out of condition.

Joe had shot his deer in the morning, only a short distance from the road. He had dressed it out and hung it up to cool while he went on hunting. When he came back for it, and it was gone, the tracks in the leaves were not clear, but there were enough there and where the deer was dragged to the car to show that only the short man was involved. Also, he had to drag a piece of an old log to where the deer was hanging to be able to reach high enough to cut the rope—a clean cut with a sharp knife.

The short rifle? While he cut down the deer, the hunter leaned his rifle against an aspin tree. The open sight cut into the bark.

How about the jeans with mud on the left knee? The car

had been parked on bare, muddy ground. When the men had lifted the deer onto the car the short man had gotten down on one knee to pick it up. Joe put his knee beside the track. The material was the same.

The tracks beside the car showed they had put the deer on top, not inside. The narrow space between the car tracks showed that it was a small foreign car. When the car turned, the summer tires of the back wheels cut a shorter circle; then when they straightened out, they covered the tracks of the studded snow tires on the front. The car had front wheel drive.

The sprinkle of rain a half hour before Joe found the deer missing was a bit of luck. It not only made the tracks plainer, it helped with the timing. Considering the time it would take the men to drag the deer to the car and tie it on, they could not have been gone more than ten minutes before Joe arrived. As a good tracker, he might have guessed the age of the tracks without the rain, but not that accurately.

The secret of being a good tracker, is observing everything, not just tracks.

E.

DEER AND OTHER HOOFED ANIMALS

The tracks of many of the deer and other hoofed animals are so much alike that you usually have to rely on clues other than the shape of the track itself to tell you which one made the track. The tracks of mule deer, whitetail deer, blacktail deer, antelope, mountain goat, bighorn sheep, domestic pig, domestic sheep, and goats are all nearly identical.

The location of the track is some help, as each animal has a preferred type of terrain, but this is not enough evidence for positive identification of the tracks, as the ranges overlap. The way the animal runs is also a help to the careful observer.

Mule Deer

The following is the track of a mule deer buck, natural size. The track of a doe *may* be slightly smaller, and it *may* be somewhat more pointed.

Mule deer run in great high jumps that carry them easily over rocks and fences.

They are easy to tell from the whitetail by their black tipped tail (which is surrounded by a white patch, and is usually held down except when the animal is alarmed), their large ears, and their antlers (which divide near the forehead, then each branch usually divides again).

The Coast Blacktail is very similar to the mule deer, but is much smaller, has smaller ears, and lives on the Coast Range of northern California and Oregon. It holds its tail straight out or swishes it back and forth.

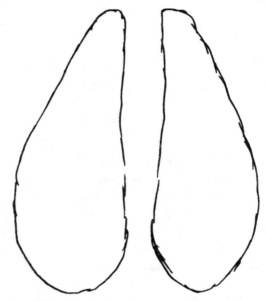

MULE DEER, MOUNTAIN BLACKTAIL: *Odocoileus hemionus*
Blackfeet: Ai-wa-ka-si
Cree: Ap-is-chick-i-koosh
Navajo: Kiih-kai (Buck)
Oglala Sioux: Tah-heenchala
Length: 6 feet plus 8 inch tail. Height 3½ feet
Range: The mule deer is the deer you are most likely to find in the high rugged areas of the Rocky Mountains. It prefers the partially wooded lower hills, but goes above timberline in summer, and also out onto the open prairie. Tracks on the open plains east of the Rockies may be either mule deer or antelope. In fall or winter an animal that is alone is more likely to be a deer.

Tracks are from Bridger Mountains, Montana.

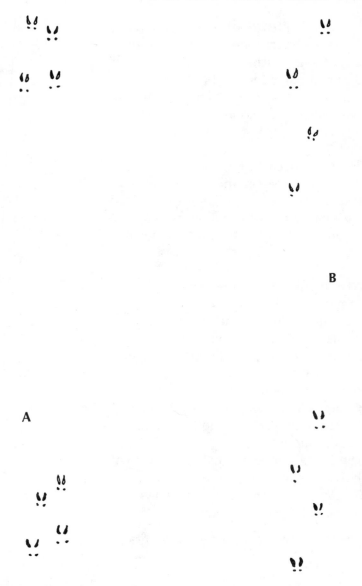

A. Mule deer running in about one inch of fresh snow. Leaps of about 10 feet. Tracks of back feet are behind those of front feet. **B.** Whitetail deer running in one inch fresh snow. About 6 foot leaps. Back feet are ahead of front. Dew claws are closer to hoofs of front feet. They usually only show in soft mud or snow.

Whitetail Deer

The whitetail are the common deer of the East, but their range overlaps that of the mule deer in the Rockies and northern plains. Whitetail deer prefer the rolling hills and mountains.

They run very much the way a horse runs.

They are easily recognized by the tail which is white on the underside, and which, when they are frightened, is raised like a flag; and by the antlers, which have one main stem, with the points branching off, forward.

WHITETAIL DEER: *Odocoileus virginianus*
Cheyenne: Vaotseva
Cree and Ojibwa: Wah-ai-ush
Oglala Sioux: Tah-keenchalah
Length: 5 feet plus 10 inch tail. Height 3 foot.
Range: Bounded on the east and south by the Atlantic, on the west by central New Mexico, central Colorado, southern Idaho, central Oregon, and central Washington. They go about 500 miles north of the U. S.–Canadian border.
The smaller Arizona Whitetail lives in Arizona and New Mexico.

Tracks shown are from central Montana.

Deer walking.

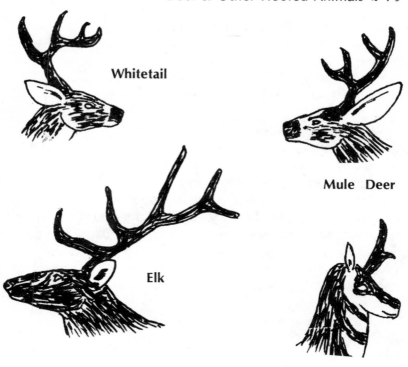

Whitetail

Mule Deer

Elk

Antelope

Mule deer. Note big ears and black tail.

Pronghorn Antelope

The track of the antelope can sometimes be distinguished from the deer when the tracks are in deep mud or snow, because the antelope has no dewclaws—the two smaller hoofs a few inches up the leg, which all of the deer family have.

The antelope is strictly a plains animal. Originally there were 30 to 40 million antelope on the western plains. By 1900 they were so scarce as to be considered an endangered species. In 1927 there were articles in several magazines predicting that within ten years antelope would be extinct because they required unfenced open range, and the open range was nearly gone. But the antelope have adapted and are again numerous. In three hours driving across eastern Wyoming, I have counted thirty herds, each of which contained 15 to 30 antelope—and this was within sight of only one highway.

During the spring and early summer antelope may be in small groups or even one or two at a time, but the rest of the year they gather together in larger herds, so if you find tracks of an animal traveling alone, it is more likely the tracks of a deer.

Antelope.

The running gait of the antelope is very smooth and very fast. It is the second fastest animal in the world. It loves to race. I watched one antelope leave its herd to race a passenger train. It ran alongside the locomotive for more than three miles before it turned back to join the herd. Another time I tried to head off a herd of antelope with my car. I was bouncing across the prairie at between 45 and 50 miles an hour, running almost parallel to the herd, assuming that when we got close enough they would turn. Instead, when we met, they just sped up and crossed in front of me.

One day I found the tracks of a herd of antelope milling around the top of a cliff which overlooked an open meadow. I wondered about the reason because it looked as if they were looking for a way down, yet they did not go down a nearby slope where it would have been easy, but turned and started grazing. I got my answer when I came by the same spot the next day. Twenty-three antelope were lined up along the edge of the cliff, watching seven mule deer playing in the meadow. The deer were chasing each other around and around, jumping back and forth over a fence. The scene characterized both animals very well: the playful mule deer, which loves to jump, and the curiosity of the antelope. The Indians used to hunt the antelope by lying down in the grass and every minute or so they would wave a piece of white buckskin over their heads for just a

Antelope running.

second. The antelope would be so curious about the flash of white, that they would approach within arrow-shot.

The pronghorn is not related to the antelope of Africa. It is a family by itself, unrelated to other animals. It has characteristics of the goat, antelope, giraffe, and deer. It has only two hoofs, without dewclaws, like the giraffe; a gall bladder, scent glands, and hollow horns on a bony core like the goat; and hair with a wool undercoat, branching horns, and sheds its horns like the deer. No other animal sheds only the outside of its horns each year.

The pronghorn antelope is easy to distinguish from the deer by its horns, the larger amount of white on its belly and the two white stripes on its neck.

PRONGHORN: *Antilocapra americana*
Cheyenne: vo'haa'e
Cree: Ah-pi-chee ah-tik (small caribou)
Oglala Sioux: Tah-heen-cha Sanla (little pale deer)
Length: 4 feet plus 3 inch tail. Height 3¼ feet.
Range: Open plains areas from western Nebraska to western Nevada and from southern Arizona to northern Montana.

Tracks shown are from eastern Montana.

Elk.

Elk

The track of the elk looks like that of the deer, only larger.

If you are following an elk trail through thick timber, a large bull will sometimes detour around a spot where two trees are too close together for his antlers.

AMERICAN ELK, WAPATI: *Cervus canadensis*
Shawnee: Wapiti
Blackfeet: Ponoka
Cheyenne: Mo'ehe
Cree: Mus-koose
Crow: Itsi-rikya-se
Oglala Sioux: Hay-hah-kah
Ojibway: Mush-koose
Length: 9 feet, 6 inch tail. Height 4½ feet.
Range: Elk once ranged from the Allegheny Mountains to the West Coast, from Tennessee to the Great Lakes, and from Oklahoma to northern British Columbia. They are now found only in the Rocky Mountains, a small area on the West Coast, and in an area in Manitoba and Saskatchewan. They have been introduced into some of the islands along the south coast of Alaska.

Moose

The moose is as large as a horse and is the world's largest member of the deer family. Its tracks are like those of the deer and elk, only larger still and somewhat more pointed, and they spread more. This helps to keep the moose from sinking into the mud of the swamps which are its preferred home. It picks its feet up higher than the domestic cow, so its tracks show less drag in deep snow.

The moose spends much of its time in the summer wading in the water, eating water plants. In winter it moves to the higher levels.

Moose cow and calf.

MOOSE: *Alces americana*
Cree: Moose
Ojibway: Moose
Cheyenne: Mahpe-mo'ehe
Dena'ina: K'uhda'i (Cook-die'a)
Sioux: Ta
Length: Alaska, about 10 feet; Montana 8 feet; tail 3 inches
Height: 6½ feet; 5½ feet.
Range: The moose is still quite common all across Canada and Alaska, and there are still a few in Montana, Idaho, Wyoming, and Maine.

Caribou

The track of the caribou is easily distinguished from the cow and the musk ox because of the long outer edge of the hoof. It is more round than that of the moose and other deer, and it spreads in snow. The caribou track shows the dewclaws only on the front feet. These show quite a distance behind the hoof tracks. The track is not easily confused with any other track unless it would be a small horse in deep snow.

The caribou is easy to distinguish from other deer by its heavier body, white neck and feet, and its magnificient antlers worn by both the males and females.

The caribou is easy to distinguish from other deer by its heavier body, white neck and feet, and the magnificent antlers which are worn by both the males and females.

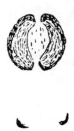

BARREN GROUND CARIBOU, *Rangifer arcticus,*
WOODLAND CARIBOU, *Rangifer caribou*

Cree: Ah-tik
Dena'ina: Vejx jook
Northern Eskimo: Took-too
Yupic Eskimo: Tun-tuq
Yankton Sioux: Tang-kah
Length: 7 feet, tail 5 inches, height 4 feet.
Range: Originally all of Canada, Alaska, and Maine, with a few in northern Minnesota and northwestern Montana and Idaho. It is now in Alaska and arctic Canada. There is a herd of woodland caribou in northern Idaho, and a small bunch near Yaak, Montana.

Tracks shown are from western Alaska. The upper track is a front foot track in 1 inch of snow. The lower is a hind foot in hard mud.

Buffalo

The track of the bison and the domestic cow look alike, but there is little chance of getting them confused, unless you are hunting a cow that has gotten onto a buffalo range, or looking for the buffalo that sometimes wander outside Yellowstone.

AMERICAN BUFFALO, BISON *Bison Bison*
Cheyenne: Bull: Hotova'a. Cow: Méhe
Chipewyan: Ed-jea-ay
Cree: Mush-kwe-tay
Crow: Chii-la-pe
Sioux: Bull: Tah-tank-kah; Cow: Ptay
Navajo: 'àyán-i (the one who eats)
Length: Up to 11 feet plus 2 foot tail. Height: 6 feet.
Range: All the buffalo are now in national parks, game preserves, or buffalo ranches.

Tracks shown are from the Black Hills.

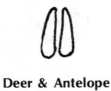

Deer & Antelope

Moose

Pig

Caribou

Domestic Cow

Buffalo

Horse

Horse

The tracks of the average horse are five to six inches across. The front feet are sightly larger than the rear feet.

Mountain Sheep and Goats

Although I have watched many mountain goats, I have never seen a clear track of one. They don't make many tracks on the high rocky crags from which they like to look down on the world.

The tracks of the bighorn sheep would also be distinguished from those of deer, mainly by the high rocky ridges that they inhabit.

The pure white dall sheep choose the same kind of location in the mountains of Alaska as their cousins, the bighorn, choose in the Rockies. In summer they show up clearly against the dark mountains, and you are much more likely to see the sheep than their tracks. Their deer-like tracks would be easy to distinguish by their location high on the mountains. They would also be much smaller than those of their only neighbors, the caribou and moose, both of which prefer the open tundra or the low wooded areas.

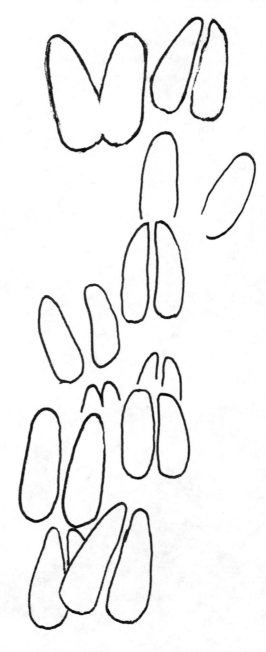

Domestic sheep tracks on a mountain trail. The tracks of one kind of animal do not all look alike.

Tapir

The tapir is a three hoofed relative of the horse and the rhinoceros, living mostly along the streams in the South American jungles. However it does get up into Central America and southern North America.

TAPIR: *Tapirella bairdi*
Yanowamo: Shama
Length: About 4 feet.
Height: Nearly 3 feet.

Tracks shown are from southern Venezuela.

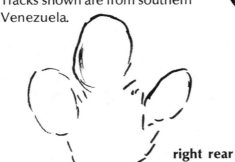

right front

right rear

6.

THE MYSTERY OF THE HUNGRY COWS

"I can't figure it out," Jim Ludke said. "I've been feeding those cows enough corn to fatten twice their number, and instead of getting fat, they keep getting thinner. They always act like they're hungry."

Don Little Fox rubbed his chin. "Could be they're not gettin' enough to eat," he said.

"But I'm feeding them twice as much as they recommend for fattening cows," Jim complained. "I can't feed them more. I had a good crop of corn so I bought those cows, and thought I'd fatten them up for market. It would be a good way to make money off my corn. But they're getting thinner instead of fatter."

The two men walked down to the feed lot to look at the cows. Two of the cows were at the feed troughs trying to lick up the few grains of corn that were left. The rest were lying by the fence at the end of the lot. "They do look a little thin," Don said.

When the cows saw the two men, they got up and came running, thinking they might get fed. Jim said "See! They act like they're half starved."

"Just run them off for a minute, so I can look around the feed troughs before they tramp around." Don walked along the feed troughs then came back laughing and asked, "Have you seen those cows eat the corn?"

Jim nodded his head. "I feed them every evening. When I leave them they are always eating as fast as they can eat."

Don thought a minute. "Put your cows in the other pasture where they can eat grass for two weeks. Then put them back in here and give them the same amount of corn. I'll guarantee they will get fat." With that he turned and walked away.

It was almost dark when Don came back carrying a big bundle of steel traps. He checked to be sure the cows were gone before he spread some corn in the feed troughs. Then he set the traps along both sides.

Don worked late each evening setting his traps, then checked them early in the morning, so Jim never saw him. But at the end of the two weeks Jim put his cows back in the feed lot and fed them corn.

A month later Don drove up in his pickup as Jim was feeding his cows. "Looks like they're gettin' fat," he said.

"They sure are," Jim said, "but what did you do? Where was my corn going?"

Can you guess Don's answer?

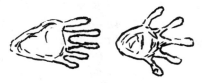

"There were raccoon tracks all over the place," Don said. "If you had kept your eyes open you would have seen them. You see, every night when you fed corn to your cows, the raccoons waited until you left, then they came running and scared the cows off. That's not hard to do when it's dark and there are plenty of raccoons. By the time the coons left there wasn't much left for the cows to eat."

"Well, I sure thank you for saving my cattle feeding business," Jim said.

"Don't thank me," Don answered with a grin. "I have 57 raccoon skins to sell!"

F.

THE BEAR, WEASEL, and RACCOON

The animals described in this chapter are all carnivorous, that is, their main food is other animals, either meat, fish, or insects. However, there is great variety among them. The opossum is the only remaining American marsupial, the ancient family of pouched animals that now live mainly in Australia. The shrew is the smallest mammal in the world, while the Alaska brown and polar bears are the world's largest meat eaters.

The Bear Family

There are four kinds of bears in America, but most people have an opportunity to see only one, or possibly two in the wild. However, anyone who might hike, camp, or hunt where there are both black bears and grizzlys needs to be able to quickly tell the difference between these two. Trying to get close enough to photograph, or trying to frighten away from camp, a "black bear" that turns out to be a grizzly could be a disaster. Also, it would be a tragedy if a hunter who was hunting black bear was to shoot a grizzly, which is an endangered species. If you are not absolutely certain, it is better to pass up a shot at a black bear than to kill a grizzly.

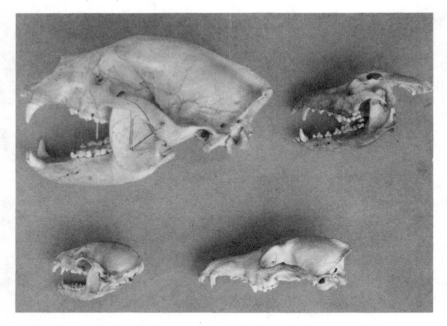

Skulls of the black bear, mountain lion, bobcat, and coyote.

Neither color nor size are reliable means of identification. A large black bear and a small grizzly may be the same size, and it is difficult to judge the size of an animal running through the forest. Although the "usual" color of the two is somewhat different, there is a great variation in the color of both. They may be anything from a light brown to black.

Compare the pictures. The black bear does not have a noticeable shoulder hump. Its highest point is its back, above the hips. The grizzly's highest point is definitely the shoulder hump.

The black bear's face is straight, and thinner than the grizzly's. Notice the eyebrow ridge on the grizzly.

In spring and fall, the grizzly has a ruff of long hair around it's neck. Typically, the grizzly has white tips on most of its hairs, giving it the "grizzled" appearance from which it got its name. This is also responsible for its other name, the "silver-tip." However this coloring does not show in some light conditions, nor is it always present. Grizzly bears range from brown

Black Bear

Grizzly Bear

Alaska Brown

to almost black. Those in northern Alaska may even be a very light gray.

The claws of the black bear are black. Those of the grizzly are light colored and much longer. You can often see them from quite a distance.

The tracks of all bears are very much alike, and you cannot usually be certain which kind they are. There are five toes on each foot, and the track of the back foot looks much like the track of a person, only much wider. If the tracks are in light snow or mud you may see some differences. The claws of the front feet of the grizzly often show, and the claw marks will be 1¾ to 4½ inches from the toe mark. The claws of the black bear seldom show in the tracks. If they do, they will not be more than 1½ inches from the toe mark. Also, the toes of the grizzly's front foot are somewhat more in a straight line across than those of the black bear.

In very clear tracks, you can also notice that there is a notch in the side of the back foot track of the black bear, making it somewhat like the track of a person with a high arch. The back of the heel is rounded. The grizzly's track is more "flat-footed" and the back appears more pointed.

The Alaskan brown bear's track is like the grizzly's, but less likely to have claw marks showing.

The average length of the track of the adult black bear is 6 to 7 inches; the grizzly, 10 to 12 inches; and the Alaskan brown bear about 14 to 17 inches. However, there is enough overlap in size of tracks, as in size of bears, so that size is not a definite identification, especially since a grizzly cub may be the same size as an adult black bear.

You will usually find only the tracks of the bear's hind feet, as the hind feet are placed in the tracks of the front feet. The tracks will be placed like a man's, but with bigger steps and a wider straddle. Unless the cubs are playing, or curiously investigating the area, the tracks of a mother and cubs may look like the tracks of one bear, as the cubs will carefully place their feet in their mother's tracks. A family of bears may make a permanent trail of separate tracks by placing their feet in the old tracks each time they follow the trail.

Black

Grizzly

Alaska Brown

Black Bear

There are two common color variations of the black bear, black and brown. They are not two species, just blonds and brunettes. Quite often a mother will have twin cubs, one brown and one black.

BLACK BEAR: *Ursus americanus*
Apache: Shaz
Blackfeet: Siko-kia-yowa
Cheyenne: Mo'otse-**nah**kohe (black) Mus-kwa (bear)
Cree: Kus-kit-**tay** (black) Mus-**kwa** (bear)
Crow: Dah-pits-e
Dena'ina: Yeghedishla
Nez Perce: Yackkah
Oglala Sioux: Mah-**to**-wag-hay
Navajo: Naa-lcoi (Yellow-eyed one)
Mexican: Oso
Length: About 5 feet.   Height: 3 feet.
Range: At one time there were black bears in nearly every part of the United States and Canada. They are still found in the national parks, national forests, and other thinly populated forest areas throughout the country.

Tracks from the Beartooth Mountains, Montana.

Grizzly Bear

When looking for grizzly tracks there are other signs you should watch for: holes where the bear has dug up ground squirrels or roots, marks where the cubs have climbed trees. (Bears love to scratch their backs.) Male grizzlys will reach as high as they can reach and scratch the bark off trees. Old-timers say these are border markings and that another grizzly will avoid the territory of a grizzly who can reach higher on the tree.

The grizzly is known for its fearlessness, which is reason for caution when in its territory. I have had black bears in my camp at least thirty times, and have chased them away at least

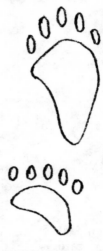

Alaska Brown Bear

Grizzly

Black Bear

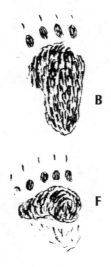

B

F

Grizzly, walking fast. At a slower gate, back foot steps in track of front foot. Heel of front foot and inner toes often do not show.

a dozen times by running at them and yelling, or throwing sticks. I have had grizzlys come to my camp only twice, and I left them alone. As one old-timer told me, "If one of you is going to get chased, it won't be the grizzly."

If you are camping in any area where there is even a remote *possibility* that there are any bears of any kind, *never* put food inside your tent. I never put mine inside even where there are no bears. As a youngster, before I learned this, I had both a skunk and a porcupine come inside my tent and go through my food supply while I was "sleeping" beside it.

In timber country it is best to put your food, especially meat, fruit, and sweets, in a sack, tie the sack to a rope, throw the rope over the limb of a tree, and pull the sack up out of the reach of any wildlife. In grizzly country I always put this away from camp. I don't want a frustrated grizzly standing in front of my tent trying to reach his meal!

I recommend that you do this before the grizzly shows up! I was once in the process of tying my rope to my food sack when a young grizzly arrived. There was no argument. I simply backed away. I was a little hungry for the rest of the trip!

Even a grizzly bear, if given a choice, would rather run than fight. If he sees you at a distance he will almost invariably run away. However, if he is surprised close up, he may think the only way to escape is to attack. When I am backpacking in grizzly country, especially in Alaska, but even in Montana, I always carry a sheep bell and a referee's whistle. In tundra country, either in the far north, or on the tops of the Rockies, I just stay out in the open where I won't surprise a bear close up. When I am in bush or timber I hang the bell from my pack to let the bears know I am coming. I also hang the whistle around my neck.

My partner on an Alaskan trip and I were just setting up camp beside a valley filled with willows. I watched a big silvertip grizzly come down the mountain on the other side of the valley. He was coming straight toward us without making one turn. When he entered the willows, I said, "If he keeps coming the same way, he'll come out of the willows not twenty feet from us." Doug grabbed his bell, and I grabbed my whistle. When we sounded the grizzly leaped into the air not thirty yards from us to look around, then tore off in the opposite direction.

Even a black bear will turn to fight or will attack if cornered or wounded, or if you get between a mother and her cubs. But this applies to almost any animal, not just bears. If you doubt it, try grabbing a young raccoon when the mother is near, shoot a bobcat with a 22, or corner a weasel in a barn. I have seen all three attack in these situations: In other words, bears, and most other animals, will fight anything to defend themselves and their families, but will not bother the person who respects their privacy, and who lives with them on a friendly basis.

GRIZZLY BEAR, SILVERTIP BEAR: *Ursus horribilis*
Blackfeet: Apii-soo-kia-yawa
Cheyenne: Vohpahtse-**nah**kohe (white mouthed bear)
Chipewyan: Klay-zy
Cree and Ojibwy: Mish-e muk-wa
Nez Perce: Hohost
Oglala Sioux: Mah-to shah-kay hanska
Tlingit: Xuts!

The grizzly.

Length: About 7 feet. Height: 40 inches.
Range: Originally from northern Mexico to Alaska and from the eastern Dakotas to the West Coast. However it is now Alaska, western Canada, and a few of the more isolated areas in the Rockies, mainly in Montana, Wyoming, and Idaho, and the high Cascades.

Tracks shown are from Yellowstone.

Alaska Brown Bear

The Alaskan browns share with polar bears the distinction of being the world's largest meat eating animals. The Alaskan brown bear (often called the Kodiak bear) is really a very large variation of the grizzly, developed in a region where food is plentiful. Their tracks, their appearance, and their temperament are very similar. to that of the grizzly. The main difference is in size. While the black bear will average 200 pounds, and the grizzly will weigh around 500, the Alaskan brown bear may weigh nearly 1000 pounds.

While the Alaskan grizzly usually has a noticeable silvery color, the Alaskan brown bear, is usually a solid brown.

ALASKA BROWN BEAR, KODIAK BEAR: *Ursus arctos middendorffi*
Dena'ina: Ghenuy
Yupic Eskimo: Taquaq
Length: About 8 feet. Height: About 4 feet. (Ten feet tall when standing on hind legs.)
Range: Alaskan brown bears live mostly on Kodiak Island, the islands of the Aleutian chain, and on the Alaska Peninsula as far north as Lake Ilianna.

Tracks shown are from Chignik Lake, Alaska.

Black bear in Montana.

Grizzly in Alaska.

Polar Bear

The polar bear is as large as the Alaska brown bear, but longer and leaner in appearance, and always white or yellowish white.

It is an excellent swimmer and lives mostly on seals and some fish. Many polar bears never go onto land, living their entire lives in the ocean on the ice floes that float there.

In winter, the female makes a den in the ice to have her young, but the male stays out all through the long arctic night.

I have never seen the track of a polar bear, but I understand that it averages about 14½ inches long, and that it is similar to a grizzly's except that the pads seldom show clearly because of the long thick fur that grows down around the feet.

POLAR BEAR: *Ursus martimus*
Eskimo: **Na**nooq
Cheyenne: **Vohpe-nah**kohe
Length: Up to 8 feet. Height: 4 feet.
Range: The range of the polar bear is mainly the Arctic Ocean. It also floats down the Berring Sea on ice floes, from which it swims back, hundreds of miles. It goes only a little way onto the land on all sides of the Arctic Ocean.

Raccoon

The raccoon, known to some tribes as "the bear's little brother," is one of the most interesting and intelligent of animals. Although the skull of the raccoon and the opossum are approximatley the same size, the raccoon's skull has approximately five times as much space for the brain.

Because of its intelligence and its nimble fingers, a raccoon can learn to open almost any latch and get in or out of almost any enclosure. And because of its curiosity it loves to get into and investigate everything.

The raccoon prefers a hollow limb high in a tree for a den, but will use any secure hollow space. Being a night animal, it seldom comes out in the daytime, except to sun.

It eats a diet much like that of humans, a combination of meat, fruit, and vegetables, with a particular fondness for fruit. It likes the water and is adept at finding and catching crayfish and all the little insects that live among the rocks in a stream. Raccoon tracks are therefore common along the banks of streams.

The tracks are often described as "like miniature bear tracks," or "like a baby with long toes." Raccoons have five toes on each foot. When they walk, they place the left hind foot beside the right front foot, so the tracks of the front and hind foot of the opposite sides are beside each other.

The raccoon makes a variety of sounds, but the most common is a chir somewhat like that of the grey squirrel but much lower in tone.

RACCOON, COON, *Procyon lotor*

Algonquian: Ratoon or Arocoun

Cheyenne: Mach-coon or Matseskome

Cree: Es-see-ban

Oglala Sioux: Wee-cha

Mexican: Mapachi

Length: About 2 feet plus 1 foot tail.

Range: Originally the southern states, but because of their adaptability raccoons have moved into inhabited areas as other carnivores moved out. They now occupy nearly every part of the United States.

Tracks from northern California.

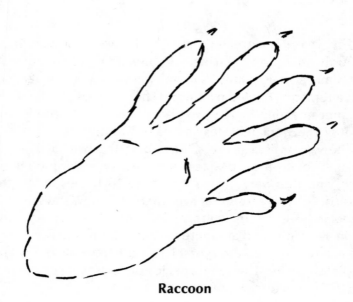

Raccoon

The Weasel Family

There is great variety in the members of the weasel family, but they are all superior hunters, very intelligent, active, and most of them are very playful. They all have scent glands that produce an odor, but the others do not use their scent for defense to the extent that the skunk does.

They all have five toes on both the front and back feet. Being long bodied and short legged, the front foot tracks often show in front of the hind foot tracks, rather than behind them as in the tracks of the cat and dog families.

I have never seen the tracks of the martin or fisher, but they would be similar to those of the mink, except that the martin is larger than the mink, and the fisher is larger still.

Weasel

The weasel is extremely active and quick. It dodges back and forth with sudden changes in direction and speed. If it does run in a straight line, its jumps will vary greatly in length, often alternating between long and short leaps, the long ones sometimes nearing six feet. The back feet usually land in the tracks of the front feet, leaving paired footprints.

The weasel is a fearless little thing that will pursue an animal several times its size. There are several varieties of weasel and they vary in size from 7 to 20 inches in length.

Most of the weasels that live where the snow stays on the ground in winter turn white in winter. The white furs are known as ermine and are quite valuable. Surprisingly it takes only a few days for the weasel to turn from all brown to completely white. The same species of weasel, when farther south, will not turn white.

WEASEL, ERMINE: *Mustela erminea* and others
Cheyenne: Xaa'e
Chipewyan: Tel-ky-lay
Cree and Ojibway: Shing-gwus
Crow: U-ute
Oglala Sioux: He-tu-**kah**-san
Length: 5 to 15 inches plus 2 to 7 inch tail.
Range: All of North America.

Tracks are from south of Medicine Hat, Alberta.

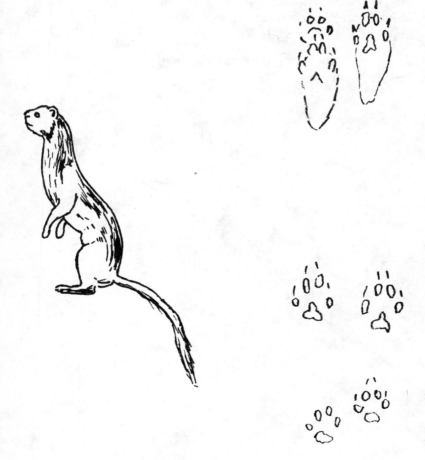

Mink

The tracks of the mink are much like those of the weasel except that they are somewhat larger. They could easily be confused with the tracks of the red fox or the house cat, except that the mink has five toes. However, the fifth toe does not always show in the track.

MINK: *Mustela vison*
Chipewayan: Tel-**chu**-say
Cree: Sang-**gwiss** or Jackashew
Ojibway: Shange-**gwes**-se
Oglala Sioux: Lo-**Chin**-cha
Length: About 18 inches plus 8 inch tail.
Range: Forested areas of northern United States, Canada, and Alaska.

Tracks and photo are from the Flathead Indian Reservation, Montana.

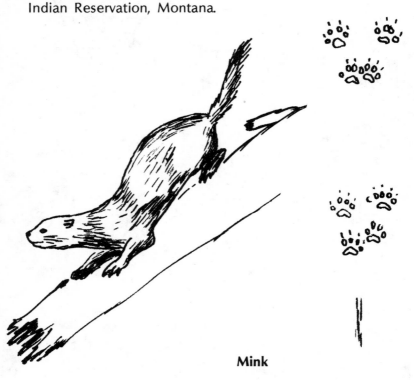

Mink

Wolverine

Multiply the size, ferocity, and cunning of the weasel by about twenty and you have the wolverine.

The wolverine's tracks can easily be confused with those of the wolf unless you can find a clear individual footprint, so that you can see the fifth toe, and the difference in the shape of the back of the foot pad. The running track patterns are similar to those of the wolf, but the tracks will be somewhat closer together.

Although the wolverine is seldom seen, and is probably the hardest of all animals to trap, most trappers go after it with a vengence. First, it loves to raid the trapline and steal either the bait from the traps or the animals that have been trapped. Second, the fur is highly valued. Wool and the furs of the wolf, coyote, and most other animals collect frost when your breath strikes them in below zero weather, and therefore are cold when next to your face, but wolverine fur does not frost, so a strip of wolverine fur next to your face on the ruff of a parka is important in arctic weather.

Unlike most animals, which kill only as much as they can eat, the wolverine will kill what it does not intend to eat. I once had to shoot a dog that had been caught in a trap and was badly mangled by a wolverine that found it in the trap.

WOLVERINE, CARCAJOU, *Gulo luscus*
French Canadian: Carcajou
Eskimo: Kap-rik
Chipewyan: Nog-gy-ay
Cree: Kin-kwa-har-gay-o or Kee-wa-har-kess
Dena'ina: Idashla (ee-dah-shla)
Yankton Sioux: Skay-cha tung-ka
Length: About 2½ feet plus 9 inch tail.
Range: Alaska, Canada, and the timberline areas or our highest western mountains. However, it is nearly gone from all the states except Alaska.

Tracks are from Lake Ilianna, Alaska.

Wolverine.

Badger

The badger looks like a small bear, flattened out, and with its face colored black and white. It is about thirty inches long, and less than half that tall.

Before you see the tracks of a badger you will probably find evidence of its presence in the holes it has dug. With its short powerful legs and long claws, it is one of the most powerful and fastest of diggers, and gets many of the small rodents upon which it lives by digging them out of their holes.

BADGER: *Taxidea taxus*
Cheyenne: Ma'**hah**ko'e
Oglala Sioux: Ho-**ka** (Bristly)
Pawnee: Chocartoosh
Mexican: Tajonis
Length: 1½ to 2 feet plus 6 inch tail.
Range: Ohio to the Rockies, Mexico to southwestern Canada.

Tracks shown are from southeastern Colorado.

Skunk

The skunk is, of course, best known for its horrible odor, which once smelled can never be forgotten. The scent is sprayed from a scent gland on the back of the tail, and is used only for defense against other animals. The skunk does not use its scent against another skunk, or an animal that it cannot see. It will usually face the enemy with its tail up ready, and stamp its feet as a warning before finally using its scent as a last resort. But once the spray is used, it is extremely effective.

The skunk is about the size of a house cat, and walks with its feet flat on the ground like the bear. It is slower, less active, and less inquisitive than the other members of the weasel family. The tracks are therefore closer together and the gait somewhat less changeable.

The skunk sleeps through the winter, but may be out in fall or spring snows.

SKUNK: *Mephitis mephitis*
Abenaki: Seganku
Cheyenne: Xaone
Cree and Ojibway: She gawk
Crow: Xue'tse
Huron: Scangaresse
Navajo: Go'li'zii
Mexican: Zorilla
Length: 18 inches plus 10 inch tail. The spotted skunk is smaller.
Range: Various kinds of skunks are found in all parts of North America except the Far North.

Otter

The otter is one of the most playful of animals and loves to slide down mud banks or snow covered slopes. It also will run and slide in the snow when traveling on the level. It does much of its winter travel under the ice of the rivers in which it spends most of its time.

All these actions plus the webbed hind foot would be distinguishing features of the trail of the otter, although the web of the foot often does not show in the tracks.

OTTER: *Lutra canadensis* (and others)
Cheyenne: Naene
Chipewyan: **Nop**-e-ay
Cree and Ojibway: Ne-**geek**
Crow: Ba-puxte
Sioux: Pe-tang or ptan
Length: About 2½ feet plus 1½ inch tail
Range: Originally along the streams and rivers of most of North America. It is now scarce even in the wilderness areas.

Tracks shown are from the Qwejack River, Alaska.

Otter front foot; life size.

The land otter.

Sea Otter

There is very little chance that you will ever see the track of a sea otter. Although I have enjoyed watching the animals I have never seen the track of one. Since they live, eat, sleep, and raise their young in the kelp beds or open ocean, they seldom come ashore.

Instead of tracks, there is another sign that will alert you to the presence of sea otters. That is the sharp sound of a seashell being tapped on a rock to break it. This sound will travel a long distance across the water. Rather than come onto shore to find a rock on which to crack the shellfish the otter eats, it will dive to the bottom, bring up a rock, and lay the rock on its belly as it floats on its back. It then holds the shell in its hands and pounds it against the rock to break it.

The sea otter was largely responsible for the exploration of the coasts of Alaska and the West Coast, as far south as northern California. Because its rich dark brown coat was the world's most valuable fur, expeditions from both Russia and the United States set out to explore the area where it lived and bring back the fur. Because of the excessive hunting, the sea otter became almost extinct. But since treaties were made with Japan and Russia totally forbidding the hunting of sea otter, it has again become fairly common. It was because the sea otters were gone that the United States was able to buy Alaska from Russia. At that time it was assumed that the fur of the sea otter and the fur of the seal were the only things of value anyone would ever get from Alaska!

Because it lives in cold water, the sea otter keeps its rich, beautiful fur all year round, and its young are born at all times of the year. But the mother has only one baby every two or three years.

SEA OTTER: *Enhydra lutris* or *Mustela lutris*
Length: Up to 3 feet plus 1 foot tail
Range: Ocean, off the shores of Alaska and California
Drawing from life, Chignik Lagoon, Alaska.

Opossum

The opossum is the only marsupial (pouched animal) native to the United States. It prefers meat, insects, and eggs, but eats fruit, tender roots, grain, and a great many other things.

In walking, the front foot track is likely to be in front of or beside the back foot track. It has five toes on each foot, and claws on all but the thumb of the back foot.

The opossum is grayish white with a white face. Its tail and toes have no fur and are flesh colored. It can use its tail to hang from a limb or carry bedding for its nest. It is well known for its ability to "play possum," that is, when it is pursued and cannot escape, it will drop over and pretend to be dead.

Opossum.

OPOSSUM, POSSUM: *Didelphis virginiana*
Algonquin: Opassum
Cheyenne: Oo'ke-va'sehe
Choctaw: Shukata
Lenape (Delaware): Much-woa-pingus
Sioux: Singteshda-tanka (big rat)
Length: About 18 inches, plus 18 inch tail
Range: Great Lakes to southern tip of
South America.

Tracks shown are from central Missouri

Armadillo

    The armadillo is covered by an armor of bony plates for protection. There is a solid front and back shield, with bands of smaller plates between. When frightened, it can roll into a ball that most enemies cannot penetrate.

    The Armadillo is an excellent digger and digs for many of the insects which are its main food. These diggings and its burrows are often easier to find than identifiable tracks.

    When I hunted with the Yanoamo Indians in South America, we would often find armadillo burrows. They would usually go down two or three feet; then run horizontally for ten to fifteen feet. We would dig a large hole to get into at the entrance, then run a long, slender, flexible sapling into the hole. While one of us wiggled the sapling around to make a noise, the other would put his ear to the ground and move around to locate the other end of the sapling. We would then dig another hole at that spot, and from there we could dig out the armadillo.

ARMADILLO: *Dasypus novemcinctus*
Spanish: Armadillo (armored, small)
Length: About 16 inches plus 14 inch tail
Range: Southern United States, Florida to Arizona and south to central South America.

Tracks shown are from east Texas.

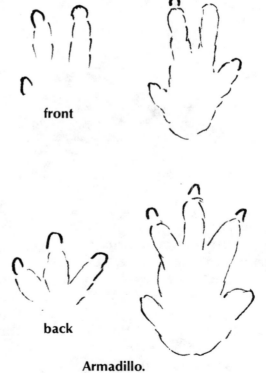

front

back

Armadillo.
Left is more typical, as other toes rarely show.

Shrew

The shrews are tiny little animals that are little known because they spend much of their time underground and come out mostly at night. Although they look somewhat like mice, and are called mice by many of the people who see them or their tracks, they are not rodents, but insect eaters.

When, as a boy, I first saw the water shrew swimming in a stream, I was told that it was a mole. Some shrews use the mole's tunnels as passageways.

The tracks of the larger shrews, such as the water shrew, are hard to distinguish from those of the field mouse, but the tracks of the four feet are in a little more of a straight line across, when it runs, so that in snow they may look like one curved line.

The tundra shrew is smaller than a mouse, which helps in identifying its tracks. The pigmy shrew, which without its tail is about one inch long, is the world's smallest mammal.

The tracks of the tundra shrew are very common among the small willows and shrubs which grow beyond the tree line in the Arctic. The tracks I have drawn show the typical change in gait of the tundra shrew as it goes from thin snow to deeper snow. The width of a set of tracks is about 1¼ inches.

PIGMY SHREW: *Microsorex hoyi*
TUNDRA SHREW: *Sorex tundrensis*
Range: There are many different species, and one or another will be found in all parts of North America.

Tracks from
Chignik Lagoon,
Alaska.

Mole

You will not find tracks, as you usually think of them, of moles. The "tracks" of moles are their runways. These are ridges of earth pushed up as the mole digs its way just under the surface. When digging farther underground, it pushes the dirt out of the hole into a molehill which, unlike the holes of other animals, has no open entrance.

The "ropes" of pocket gophers look very much like the

Evidence of the mole.

mole's runways. If you find the ridge in mid-summer and it has a hole inside, which is partly underground, as in the photo, it is a mole's runway. If you find the rope of earth, about two inches in diameter, when the snows are melting in the spring, if it lies on top of the ground, if it is in the Rocky Mountains, and if it is solid earth with no hole, it is the work of the pocket gopher. The gopher makes tunnels through the snow, then as it digs into the ground it pushes the dirt out into the snow tunnel. When the snow melts, this leaves long ropes of earth that are usually mistaken for mole runways.

Pocket gophers and shrews are often mistaken for moles simply because they dig underground tunnels (and also use the tunnels dug by moles) but their appearance is very different. Moles have solid bodies, strong short legs with wide shovel feet for digging, pointed hairless noses for feeling and smelling their way in the underground darkness, miniature eyes, and soft silky fur.

WESTERN MOLE: *Scapanus latimanus*
Length: About 5 inches plus 3 inch tail.
Range: Western mole and shrew mole: Pacific coast states. Eastern mole: East Coast to western plains. Star-nosed mole: Along waterways of eastern states.

7.

MYSTERY OF THE EMPTY BOTTLES

I was eleven years old, and I was excited because this was my first night in a big city. My family was staying in a downtown hotel in Denver. I woke up about five o'clock in the morning, and looking out the window, saw about two inches of fresh snow. I dressed and hurried down to the street. The sidewalks already had tracks of several people, but two sets of tracks turned into an alley. I followed them. There was nothing in the alley except the tracks in the snow and some boxes of empty bottles behind the three taverns in the block.

I drew the tracks I found in that alley, as nearly as possible the way I saw them. Look at the tracks and see if you can solve these problems:

There had been two men and two animals in that alley since the snowfall. Were they all there at different times or were they all there at the same time?

Is there any indication of why either of the men was there? What did the animals do?

Study the tracks and answer the questions before you look at my answers.

Man number one is stopping at each box of bottles. Did you notice his unsteady walk? The snow had been knocked from the tops of all the boxes. Evidently he was checking all

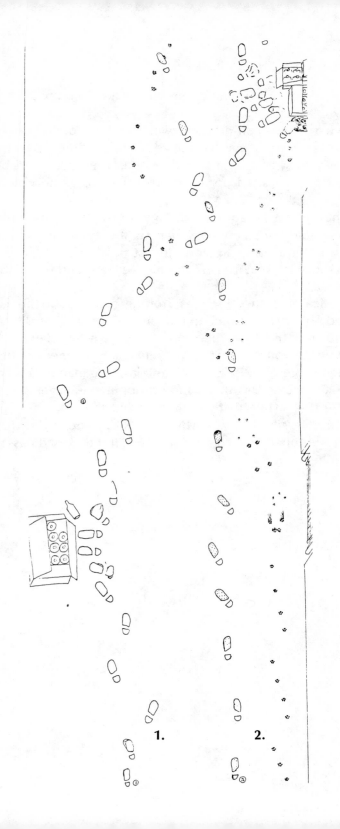

1. **2.**

the wine bottles; draining any that were not completely empty.

What about man number two? Did you notice how he watched number one as he walked by him, evidenced by the way he turned a little in that direction? Then you probably noticed that he sped up, taking longer steps as he walked away.

The cat which had been sitting next to one of the boxes was probably first alarmed by man number two. Therefore, it started off at a slow run, and did not run fast until the dog started after it. Then it made three large leaps and went over the fence.

Notice that the dog was trotting along until the cat jumped out, then it leaped in pursuit, slid to a stop as the cat jumped over the gate, then loped on down the alley.

How can you be sure this happened at the same time that the men came by? Which was made last, the man's tracks or the dog's tracks? Did the man and dog meet? Where?

The dog swung to the side to avoid the man, but you could not be sure this was why he moved aside, if they had not both stepped in each other's tracks after they had passed each other.

G.

BIRDS, REPTILES, and INSECTS

Not all of the tracks you find will be the tracks of mammals. Birds, reptiles, and insects all make tracks. So do cars and bicycles. Although you will not often try to follow the trails of anything but mammals, it is interesting to see if you can also identify the other tracks that you see. These tracks may inform you of the presence of other kinds of animal life of which you were not even aware.

Birds

There are few chances to track birds over long distances to learn their habits as you can with mammals. Flightless birds do not live where there is much snow, and birds like the wild turkey and the pheasant spend less time on the ground in winter than in the summer.

There are two main places where you will find the tracks of birds. There are always many tracks of shore and water birds on sandy ocean beaches, and sometimes on the mud or sand banks of lakes and streams. You may also find bird tracks in snow where there is food near the ground.

Water Birds

The feet of swimming birds are usually fully webbed. The feet of wading birds are also often partially webbed to keep them from sinking into soft mud. However, like the webbed feet of the otter and beaver, the webs on the feet of birds often do not show in the tracks of the bird unless they are in soft mud or fresh snow. Like the other tracks in this book, I have chosen some of the best that I have found, rather than the typical tracks, which are usually not as distinct or complete.

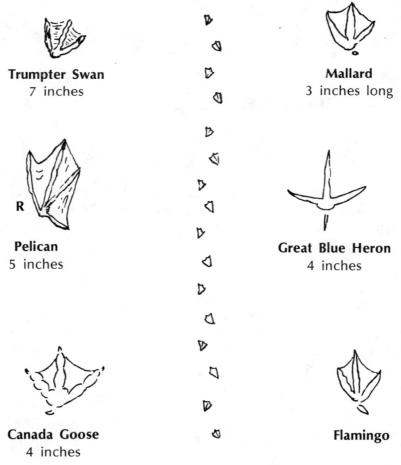

Trumpter Swan
7 inches

Mallard
3 inches long

Pelican
5 inches

Great Blue Heron
4 inches

Canada Goose
4 inches

Flamingo

Wood Duck

Tree Birds

Birds which spend most of
their time in trees usually hop
when on the ground.

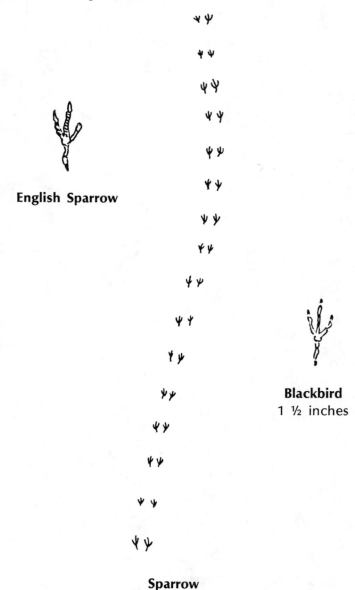

English Sparrow

Blackbird
1 ½ inches

Sparrow

Tree and Ground Birds

Birds which spend equal time in trees and on the ground both walk and hop.

Robin

Mourning Dove

Walking Birds

Birds which spend most of their time on the ground usually walk.

Wild Turkey
5 ½ inches

Chicken
4 ½ inches

Ptarmigan
2 inches

Roadrunner
3 inches

Ringnecked Pheasant
3 ½ inches

Ruffed Grouse
1 ¾ inches

Common Snipe

Bobwhite
1 ½ inches

Shore Lark
1 ½ inches

Wilson's Phalarope

Climbing Birds

The flicker and the woodpecker have two toes forward and two back so they can walk up and down a tree trunk.

Flicker
natural size (1 ¾ inches)

Birds of Prey:

Bald Eagle
6 inches

Rough Legged Hawk
right

Snowy Owl
4 inches

Screech Owl
3 inches

Great Horned Owl
4 inches, left

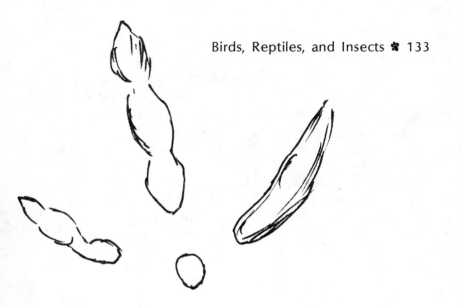

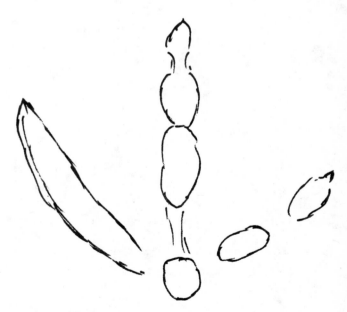

Tracks of the crow, life size.

Reptiles and Amphibians

Reptiles and amphibians have short legs on the sides of their bodies which do not hold them far off the ground—or they may have no legs at all. Therefore, they almost always show the marks of their bodies in their tracks. Since they are all cold blooded animals which cannot move when they are cold, they have to hibernate in the winter so you will not find their tracks in the snow. Nor will you find them, even in summer, in the colder climates like Alaska or northern Canada.

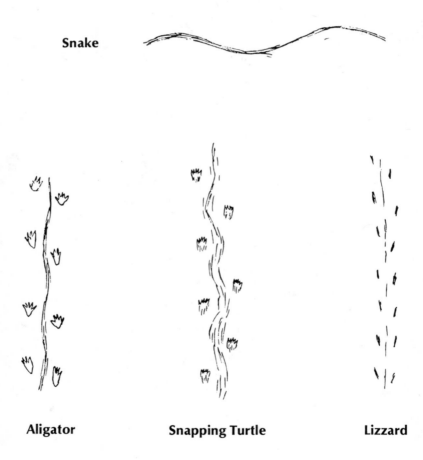

Snake

Aligator   **Snapping Turtle**   **Lizzard**

Toad   **Frog**

Amphibians

Insects and other Arthropods

Insects are also warm weather animals, so you will not find their tracks in snow either. However it is interesting to study their trails in dust or fine sand. Sea animals which come ashore, such as the sand crabs and hermit crabs, also reveal their presence by tracks in the sand.

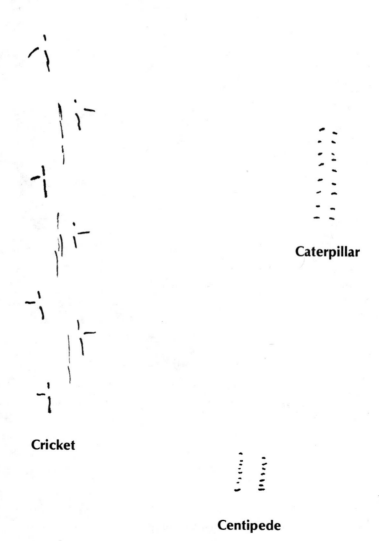

Caterpillar

Cricket

Centipede

8.

LEARNING TO TRACK LIKE AN INDIAN

American Indians have always been among the world's great trackers. The pioneers knew that Indian trackers could follow the trail of an animal or a man across hard or rocky ground where others could see no sign that anything had passed.

There are still some great Indian trackers. Scientists looking for rare species of animals often rely on Indian trackers to help them locate their quarry. Police use Indian trackers to recapture convicts.

Native people usually become better trackers than other people because they have the patience to practice, and because they are good at observing. They learn by seeing, while most other people learn more easily by hearing. However, anyone can learn to observe.

Not everyone can learn to track like an old-time Apache, but everyone can have fun learning to track, and everyone can learn a great deal about the animal life around them by observing tracks and learning about them.

No one can make you a tracker. Reading tracks is like reading words. You can only become good at it by practice. The secret of becoming a tracker is good observation—developing the habit of seeing every detail, and you can only develop that through practice.

If you have an interest in wild animals and their tracks,

don't miss the opportunity to get out the day after a fresh snowfall, especially the first snow in autumn, when some animals which hibernate later are still out. Find a track and stay with it. You will find it very worthwhile to follow one animal for several hours. If you haven't done it before, you will be amazed at the things you learn about the animal, its interests, and its way of life.

In addition to watching for the tracks of animals in the snow, or in mud, sand, and dust, watch for all the other signs of animal life.

In the woods, study the leaves on the ground. Leaves which have been recently turned over or uncovered will be darker. Watch for broken twigs. In dense forest they may be the only trail. The way the twigs break will tell you which way the person or animal was going. You may be able to follow a trail a long distance by bent twigs alone.

In long grass you will see blades bent over in the direction the animal was moving. If the grass is shorter, you may not be able to see any sign of a trail close up, but if you look quite a distance ahead, the grass that has been bent when it was stepped on will reflect the light differently. If an object was dropped onto the grass and has been there only a short time, the grass beneath it will have a darker green color, but if it has been there for several days, the grass under it will be yellow.

In dry sand a trail will be a series of dents, not tracks. If there is a breeze, the trail will be less distinct—distinguishable only by the relative position of the dents.

Fences are good places to look for tracks. Chipmunks, marmots, and bobcats use rail fences for pathways. When a mule deer comes to a barbed wire fence it jumps over easily. When an antelope comes to the same fence it turns and follows it or crawls through. When anything crosses over, through, or under a barbed wire fence, the effort usually causes it to make distinct tracks, as well as possibly leaving identifying hair or threads on the barbs.

When you find some good footprints near camp, go back and observe the same tracks several times during the day, and again the next day, to see how they have changed. Look early in the morning, after a shower, and when the sun comes out.

Indian trackers often assigned a "student" the job of sitting all day and watching a set of tracks in mud or sand to see how they changed as the sun dried the morning dew or frost, and how and when the sides began to crumble. After doing this frequently, in various kinds of weather, the boy could tell what time of day the track was made and how long it had been there.

Try to observe the changes in snow tracks also. Note how sun or wind distorts the tracks and makes them grow larger, so a deer track may look like an elk track.

Tracks of the same animal may look quite different in snow, mud, and dust.

Try to learn to identify the animal from only parts of the tracks. This is often all you will find. Remember that the toes may not all show in the track. The tracks of the front feet may be quite different from the tracks of the back feet.

Look for all the different signs that will help you identify the animal, like chewed bark, the food it has eaten, the droppings. Droppings of the same animal will be different according to the season, the food it has eaten, and its age. White stains on rocks may be from either woodrats or birds.

Try to identify every track, but when you can't, remember that even expert trackers and professional naturalists are sometimes stumped.

The old-time Indian learned every detail of every track and kept them all in his head. But most of us do not have the time or the visual memory that is needed for this. We can learn the tracks better if we record them in some way. To draw a track we have to look at every detail, and putting those details on paper helps us remember them.

When you hike or backpack, carry a sketch pad, a pencil, and a small tape measure. When you sketch the tracks you find, make your drawings either the exact size of the track or to scale. Measure the size of the tracks and also record the distance between them.

Photographs and plaster casts are other good ways of recording tracks. Although both systems give you a more exact record of the tracks, they do not help you remember the details the way drawing does. And they require more equipment. However, you should try them also. If you have a good camera that will take close-up pictures, take it with you when you are looking for tracks. But don't leave your pencil at home. Remember that white tracks in the white snow may not show up well in a photo, and you still need to record the size and location of the tracks.

Try making plaster casts also. Keep a jar of plaster of Paris handy, and when you go out to look for tracks, take some along. The technique of making good plaster casts is not difficult to learn.

Find a good clear track like this track of a wolf. Put a little plaster of Paris in a can and mix in enough water to make a mixture like pancake dough. Pour this into the track. It may take a trial or two to learn how thick to make the plaster. If the